D0854331

MANET

PHAIDON

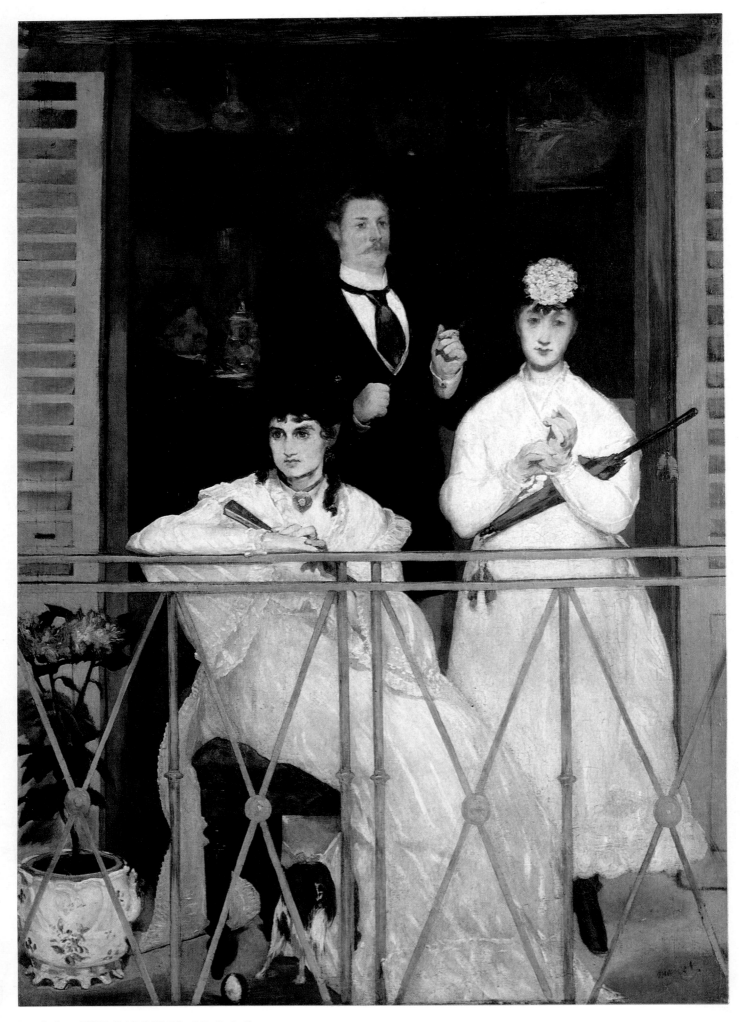

Frontispiece: THE BALCONY. 1868. Paris, Louvre

MANET

BY JOHN RICHARDSON

WITH FIFTY PLATES IN FULL COLOUR

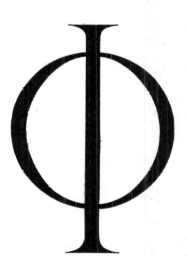

PHAIDON·LONDON·NEW YORK

ALL RIGHTS RESERVED

BY PHAIDON PRESS LTD · 5 CROMWELL PLACE · LONDON SW7

FIRST PUBLISHED 1967

SECOND IMPRESSION 1969

PHAIDON PUBLISHERS INC · NEW YORK

DISTRIBUTORS IN THE UNITED STATES: FREDERICK A. PRAEGER · INC

111 FOURTH AVENUE · NEW YORK · N.Y. 10003

LIBRARY OF CONGRESS CATALOG CARD NUMBER: 67-29886

SBN 7148 1313 3

MADE IN ENGLAND

TEXT PRINTED BY HUNT BARNARD & CO. LTD., AYLESBURY, BUCKS

PLATES PRINTED BY HUNT BARNARD & CO. LTD., AYLESBURY, BUCKS

EDOUARD MANET

CLARITY, candour, urbanity and a virtuoso ability to handle paint – such are the qualities which first strike us in Manet's art. Here, we feel, is an *oeuvre* which raises no aesthetic problems and demands no special knowledge, which can be enjoyed effortlessly, for its own sake and on its own merits. And yet how wrong our first impressions are! For underneath its bland surface Manet's art abounds in pitfalls and contradictions, so much so that none of the writers who have tried to analyse it agree on the master's special qualities or failings, and his rightful place in the hierarchy of the great is still disputed. At various times, Manet has been described as 'a frightful realist' (Gautier) and as someone 'unfortunately marked by romanticism from birth' (Baudelaire); as the artist 'who opened up the age we call modern times' (Bataille) and as 'the last of a race . . . the culminant figure who rounds off the classical tradition' (Florisoone); as the 'great master of the Impressionists' (Simon Boubée) and as 'a great painter for whom Impressionism was a deplorable aberration' (Roger Fry); as 'the most astonishing virtuoso of the modern school' (Colin) and as 'uninspired', 'mediocre' and 'mechanical' (Zervos); as a 'prince of visionaries' (Paul Mantz) and as 'totally without imagination' (Florisoone and others); as 'a revolutionary to end all revolutionaries' (Cochin), but also as 'nothing of a revolutionary, not even a rebel' (Colin) and as a '*sale bourgeois*' 'consumed by a vulgar ambition for "honours"' (Clive Bell). Now, although some of these opinions are patently ridiculous, many undeniably contain a modicum of truth.

The task of reconciling the various anomalies and of distinguishing a coherent pattern in Manet's development is far from easy. It becomes possible, however, if we realize that there is a deep-seated dichotomy in Manet's character and that the artist, like the man, has more than a single face: he was both a devoted and domesticated husband as well as an impenitent *coureur*; a pious Catholic as well as a sceptical humanist; waspish wit as well as kind-hearted friend; a gullible innocent as well as a cunning schemer; an ardent Socialist as well as a conforming bourgeois; a hard-working artist as well as an elegant *flâneur* 'who adored the *monde* and derived a secret thrill from the brilliant and scented delights of evening parties' (Zola). This does not mean that Manet was a hypocrite. He was intellectually too honest. Nor was he a schizophrenic, since his personality, though protean, was well integrated. Rather was he a Janus-like figure looking forwards and backwards simultaneously; but Janus, we should remember, was a God of beginnings, and in the last resort it is always the forward-looking rebel in Manet who triumphs over the backward-looking bourgeois.

True, Manet aspired to be an officially recognized master like Ingres. He was proud of tracing his artistic lineage back to Giorgione and Titian, though no further – earlier European art was 'barbarous'. He was also one of the last great artists to work in terms of individual set-pieces rather than in series of variations on a given theme (like Degas, Monet and the Impressionists); and by the same token he persisted, unlike other independent artists, in submitting his works to official exhibitions, because, as he said, 'the Salon is the real field of battle. It is there that one must take one's measure.' To this extent he conformed to the pattern of the past. And yet Manet loathed academicism, partly because it falsified the image in the mirror which, he felt, art ought to hold up to contemporary life; and partly because he felt that the tradition of the old masters had ceased to be valid and that a new style based on a synthesis of old and new elements was needed. Before his time the German Nazarenes and the Pre-Raphaelites had come to similar conclusions and had tried to lead the way back to the 'primitivism' of Fra Angelico and Piero della Francesca. But the members of these movements had never managed to transcend their hidebound, antiquarian ideas and so had failed to reform XIXth-century art. Manet, on the other hand, succeeded because, like most of the greatest modern innovators – Monet, Van Gogh, Cézanne, Matisse, Picasso and Braque – he was primarily an artist, not a theorist with preconceived notions of ideal beauty. In art the best results are achieved by intuitive rather than intellectual processes. Moreover, the synthesis of opposites which was at the root of his character helped Manet to fuse seemingly irreconcilable elements – taken from Daumier, the Spanish and Venetian masters, contemporary photographs and engravings, Frans Hals, Japanese wood-engravings and many other sources – into a viable modern style. It is thus a mistake to see Manet as 'the last of a race'. But is he the first of the moderns'? Here we must be careful to do full justice to Courbet, who was among the first to see that not only morally elevating subjects taken from history, legend or religion, but anything, no matter how humble and ordinary, is worthy of an artist's attention. This was to revolutionize the artist's approach to subject-matter, just as Manet's discoveries were to revolutionize the artist's approach to style. We should try to see Manet and Courbet together as twin begetters of the modern movement.

Manet's duality of temperament accounts for all kinds of paradoxes in his life, for instance a statement which he made in 1867 apropos an exhibition of some of his most controversial works: 'M. Manet has never wanted to make a protest . . . He claims neither to have overthrown the art of the past nor to have created a new order.' This, however, is exactly what he had done, but it would be a mistake to conclude that these words were insincere or disingenuous. To some extent of course Manet was out to allay the suspicions of the public, as we can guess from the advice he gave to the Impressionists some years later: 'Instead of huddling together in a separatist group, you should carry the battle into the enemy's camp. The bourgeois is under the impression that you do not exhibit at the Salon because your work will not be accepted. You should put on a tail-coat and go out into the world. Why always slop about in slippers?' Principally, however, Manet's words were dictated by the conformist side of his nature, by that side which aspired to official recognition and which – fortunately for his art – never managed to prevail. Not that Manet's conformist side was as black as it has been painted; the legend of the *sale bourgeois* who failed to live up to the genius thrust upon him by fate, dies hard. Far from being 'consumed by a vulgar ambition for "honours"[1] . . . and praise', Manet could not bring himself to give his art a different look or make the concessions which officialdom expected of him. It is also too easily forgotten that Manet was an exceptionally cultivated and sensitive man with a profound knowledge of literature and music – is it not significant that he was the intimate friend of two of the greatest poets (Baudelaire and Mallarmé) of the century? – and that he came from one of those austerely high-minded and pious families which traditionally provided the French State with the most eminent of its public servants. From his father, a distinguished jurist, and his mother, an amateur musician, Manet inherited his judicial detachment, his sure taste, his moral courage, his sharp intelligence and the toughness of spirit that sustained him through eight years of intense training and throughout his subsequent struggles. He also inherited from his parents a desire for conventional

[1] Manet in any case declared that Second Empire 'honours' were worthless.

success, though there was nothing opportunist or self-seeking about this. Manet was not out to win recognition for himself but for his work, and until this had been accorded he could see no hope for modern art.

So much for Manet the conformist: now for the rebel. The fact that the artist was all his life a convinced left-wing Republican, a bitter enemy of the Second Empire and a firm friend of men like Gambetta, Jules Ferry and Zola, is usually passed over in silence. No doubt, the treatment meted out to Manet by the Emperor's artistic advisers strengthened his views; on the other hand, we must remember that, at the age of 16, he was already inveighing against the prospect of Napoleon's election and that he was deeply affected, as a youth, by the Revolutions of 1848 and 1851 – events which he experienced at first hand and even depicted (his drawing of the fallen heroes of the barricades, described by Proust, has not survived). Because he disliked parading his private feelings, Manet's work seldom reflects his political convictions. There are, however, certain paintings which we cannot fully appreciate without taking these into consideration: notably *L'Exécution de Maximilien* (Plate 17). Various authorities have made heavy weather of the fact that in all save the first of the four versions of this composition the firing-squad is dressed in French and not Mexican uniforms; but, as Mr. Martin Davies has pointed out, if this was deliberate – and surely it was – the 'composition becomes inescapably a criticism of French policy in Mexico'. One might go even further: besides enabling Manet to pin the blame for the tragedy at Queretaro on the French, this device was also intended as an oblique comment on the plight of yet another victim of the Imperial régime – Manet himself.

Manet never made any secret of his political sympathies, so it is not surprising that during the Commune – like Corot, Courbet and Daumier – he was elected to the *Fédération des Artistes de Paris*. True, this occurred while Manet was absent from Paris and when he returned, during the last days of the Commune, he held aloof from the organization, because he was out of sympathy with extremist elements; however, a few drawings and lithographs of barricade scenes in a less detached vein than usual bear witness to his horror at the atrocities committed by the advancing army. After the Commune, Manet had hopes of expressing his liberal feelings in portraits of Victor Hugo and of his friend and hero Gambetta speaking in the Chambre des Deputés, but the statesman was too busy to spare more than two sittings – both unproductive – and Manet complained to Proust that, although Gambetta was more advanced than most, Republicans were reactionaries when it came to art. (In the following year it was Manet who refused the Republicans a favour: a request on the part of Gambetta's friend, Joseph Reinach, to allow the local Republicans to have a protest meeting in his studio, on the grounds that the artist was so 'devoted to their cause'.) No less abortive were Manet's dealings with the Municipality of Paris. For when in 1879 he wrote offering to fresco the walls of the Council Chamber in the new Hôtel de Ville with a series of socially significant scenes of Parisian markets, railways, docks, race-courses and parks (his theme, *Le Ventre de Paris*, was borrowed from Zola) and to do an allegorical ceiling painting representing all the great Frenchmen of the time, he never received an answer. With Henri Rochefort – the *communard* journalist who had made a sensational escape by boat from a penal colony – Manet had better luck: he persuaded him to sit for his portrait (Plate 42) and painted two pictures celebrating his exploit. That Manet should make a hero out of this notorious revolutionary was shocking enough; that he should then submit his portrait to the Salon of 1881 struck his friends as the act of a madman, since it nearly lost him the Salon medal and *Légion d'Honneur*, which he had always coveted and which were at long last within his grasp. But it is characteristic of Manet that he did not play for safety in politics any more than in art.

7

Like his political opinions, Manet's revolutionary approach to art declared itself at an early date. He is said to have loathed school; even drawing-lessons, arranged by his kindly Uncle Fournier, bored him so much that he took to making caricatures instead of studies after plaster-casts and had to be expelled from the class. History paintings, which Manet was also expected to copy, struck him as absurd anachronisms and, while still at school, the boy announced that Diderot was talking nonsense when he maintained that an artist should not paint a man in contemporary dress: 'One must be of one's time,' said Manet, 'and paint what one sees.' Already in youth, he showed considerable strength of character. When his formidable father tried to force him to follow a legal career, he insisted on becoming a naval cadet and when, in 1850, he failed his naval exams, he persuaded his father to allow him to study art under Couture. The best description of Manet at this period is by Antonin Proust, a fellow-pupil in the same studio and the artist's lifelong friend. Manet, he says, was of 'medium height and muscular build. He had a lithe charm which was enhanced by the elegant swagger of his walk. No matter how much he exaggerated his gait or affected the drawl of a Parisian urchin, he was never in the least vulgar. One was conscious of his breeding . . . Few men can have been as seductive as he was . . . Paris can never have produced such a *flâneur*, let alone a *flâneur* to such good purpose. As soon as the days drew in . . . and work became impossible in the studio we would rush off to the *boulevards extérieurs*. There he would jot down the slightest impressions – a profile or a hat – and when the next day a student leafing through his sketchbook would say, "you ought to finish that", Manet would roar with laughter; "you take me for a history-painter," he would say.'

Manet's relationship with Couture is something of a mystery. Certainly it was uncomfortable, but it is difficult to believe that Manet had as much contempt for his master as he later claimed. For he not only studied under Couture for six years, but ended by developing a style based on that of his master, as for instance in the early *Portrait d'Antonin Proust* (Arthur Sachs Collection, New York) and in *L'Enfant aux Cerises* (Plate 1), a pastiche that recalls, among much else, the study of a boy painted by Couture in 1846. On his side, Couture – an arrogant, bitter, irascible man – resented the ascendancy which his brilliant pupil won over the more independent students (among them Feuerbach) by laughing at his methods, by jeering both at the academic poses of the models ('do you stand like that when you buy a bunch of radishes at the greengrocer's?') and at their perpetual nakedness (when Manet persuaded a model to pose in his street-clothes, Couture said, 'my poor boy, you will never be anything but the Daumier of your time'), by mocking at history-painting and by undermining confidence in the *Prix de Rome* ('We are not in Rome and we don't want to go there. We are in Paris; let us stay there'). The trouble was that Couture, who is too seldom given credit for his many liberal and anti-academic ideas, had an unreasoning hatred of realism, as witness his satirical painting of a student drawing a pig's snout (*The Realist*; ex Coll. Vanderbilt, New York). Now Manet, who admired his master up to a point, sincerely believed that Couture would eventually come round to accepting the realist vision, and it was not until 1859, when he submitted *Le Buveur d'Absinthe* (Plate 2), his first truly realist painting, for Couture's approval that he suddenly realized his great mistake. 'There is only one absinthe-drinker here,' was Couture's comment, 'the painter who perpetrated this madness.' To our eyes *Le Buveur d'Absinthe* appears harmless enough, but it is not difficult even now to imagine how scandalous its bold simplifications, squalid Baudelairean subject-matter and obviously Daumier-like style must have appeared to a disciple of Baron Gros. Manet, however, was prepared for none of this, and it came as a horrid awakening to find that he had forfeited Couture's goodwill for ever. As a result, his feelings for his former master turned to hatred and he set about expunging the last traces of his influence from his style.

Le Buveur d'Absinthe was both the cause of Manet's final rift with Couture and the occasion of his first brush with officialdom, for it was rejected by the Salon Jury in 1859. This was a further blow to Manet, who made up his mind to choose a less controversial subject for the next exhibition. In the winter of 1860–61 Manet embarked on a large composition of a nude in a landscape (there is a preliminary sketch in the National Gallery, Oslo) based on an engraving by Vorsterman after Rubens. Although apparently destined for the Salon, this canvas did not in the end please the artist, who abandoned it and sent instead two paintings which he had completed earlier in the year: the portrait of his parents (Fig. 5) and *Le Guitarrero* (Plate 3). To Manet's delight, both paintings were accepted by the Jury, *Le Guitarrero* was awarded a medal (2nd class) and it was sufficiently well received by the critics for the artist to imagine that he had begun to make his reputation. As Alphonse Legros and Fantin-Latour were perspicacious enough to see, *Le Guitarrero* 'was painted in a strange new manner . . . halfway between realism and romanticism'. Indeed, so naturalistic was the artist's approach to his subject that, in the words of Théophile Gautier, 'this guitar-player would cut a poor figure in a romantic lithograph'. Another admirer of this work, Hector de Callias, mentioned it in the same breath with Courbet, but Courbet's rendering of a similar subject (Coll. Edith Wetmore, New York) painted sixteen years earlier, appears anecdotal and fustian beside *Le Guitarrero*.

Surprisingly, no critic seems to have detected Manet's one stylistic innovation – the elimination of half-tones – which justifies us in regarding *Le Guitarrero*, and, to a lesser extent, the double portrait as sign-posts for the future development of XIXth century art. Instead of being steeped in the ochreous, old-masterish – or, as Manet called it, 'gravy-like' – penumbra common to most Salon exhibits, this onion-eating, wine-swigging guitarist is bathed in a harsh, flat light which makes him startlingly real. Although this revolutionary approach to tonal representation had not manifested itself previously in his work, Manet had been working towards it for some years. As early as 1853 he had criticized Couture's excellent, somewhat Courbet-like *Portrait de Mademoiselle Poinsot* (National Galerie, Berlin) as being 'too encumbered with half-tones', thereby attacking one of the fundamental tenets of academic teaching: that a painting should be based on a gamut of intermediary tones, alternately hot and cold, which progress from dark to light and are keyed, like a musical composition, to a *nuance dominante*. At first Manet had difficulty in freeing his painting from the toils of this theory – for all its dramatic *chiaroscuro*, *Le Buveur d'Absinthe* is still painted in half-tones – but in *Le Guitarrero* the strong tonal contrasts achieve an effect of almost flash-lit brilliance. By exploding the fallacy of half-tones keyed to a *nuance dominante*, Manet established the artist's right to paint in whatever colours or tonalities he liked and thus enormously facilitated the development of Impressionism and much subsequent art. Small wonder that by the end of 1861 Manet found himself surrounded by a small but enthusiastic band of young artists – Legros, Carolus-Duran and Fantin-Latour among others – who looked up to him as a new master!

1862 is a crucial year for Manet's development. In a bid to consolidate his success of 1861, the thirty-year-old artist embarked on a series of ambitious paintings. According to Tabarant, the first of these is the large *Vieux Musicien* (Plate 4), a setpiece inspired by Velazquez' *Topers*, which Manet had not yet seen but which he knew at second-hand from Goya's engraving. Despite the rich, fresh beauty of its paint, *Le Vieux Musicien* is not altogether successful, for it is evidently pieced together out of separate studies; and although individually some of the figures are magnificent, others are uncomfortably derivative, notably the central group consisting of a pastiche of the boy in Velazquez' *Water-carrier* (Apsley House, London) who has his arm round the neck of a younger brother of Watteau's *Gilles*. There seems to be no spatial, temporal or compositional, let alone thematic, relationship between the figures. These faults recur in many of Manet's works of the 1860's, and for a reason that is not hard to find: Manet's sense of design was faulty. Now instead of disguising this weakness, as a less independent artist might have done, by making judicious use of the compositional formulae taught in art-schools, Manet repeatedly drew attention to it by dispensing with all but the most summary indications of perspective and by trying to reproduce on his canvas the informal – or, as he called them, 'naïve' – groupings of everyday life. This was courageous, but a number of his figure-compositions – especially those, like *Le Vieux Musicien*, consisting of a row of casually placed figures – disintegrate. As a result, the spatial illusion is often flawed by a further habitual weakness, an erratic sense of scale: e.g. the disproportionate woman in the background of *Le Déjeuner sur l'Herbe* (Plate 8), the minuscule boy in the foreground of *L'Exposition Universelle* (1867 National Gallery, Oslo) and the gigantic man with the sunshade in *La Plage de Boulogne* (1869 ex Pleydell-Bouverie Collection, London). True, Manet was a tremendously spontaneous painter who 'hurled himself on his bare canvas in a rush, as if he had never painted before' (Mallarmé); hence the freshness and unlaboured virtuosity of so many passages in his paintings, hence the clumsiness and shortcomings of others. But even when he took the precaution of making preliminary sketches, he was apt to end up with a poorly articulated design, especially if the composition involves a degree of recession or includes two or more isolated figures or groups. Sometimes, therefore, Manet would resort to improvisation; sometimes he would reduce the pictorial recession to a minimum, limiting his composition to a simple frieze-like arrangement; at other times he would search the works of older masters (Raphael, Titian, Velazquez, Chardin or Goya) for groupings which he could reverse or otherwise adapt. But on several occasions there was nothing for it but to carve up his composition – for instance, *Les Gitanos*, originally an upright *pendant* to *Le Vieux Musicien*, and *L'Épisode d'un combat de Taureaux* (1863) – into separate pictures.

In *Le Ballet Espagnol* (Fig. 2), painted later in 1862, Manet again tried to capture the haphazard grouping of real life, this time disposing his figures in a horizontal row across the canvas, in the manner of *Les Petits Cavaliers* (Louvre), a picture formerly attributed to Velazquez and which Manet had recently copied (Fig. 1). But even this simple effect eluded him and again the figures, though individually remarkable, are disproportionate and unsatisfactorily related to each other. Further examples of Manet's compositional difficulties are easily found, but this discussion of them may well end on a contrast of two large figure paintings, both of Spanish subjects and of 1862. The composition of *Lola de Valence* (Plate 7) is wholly successful; the pose, of course, derives from Goya and the setting has been taken over from a Daumier lithograph (*Dire . . . que dans mon temps, moi aussi, j'ai été une brillante Espagnole . . .* of 1857); but the different elements are perfectly adjusted and the scenery is cleverly used to enhance the back-stage reality as opposed to the romantic illusionism of the theatre. Not so the setting of *Mlle. Victorine en costume d'espada* (Fig. 4); here, too, Manet has drawn on Goya, but his sense of scale has let him down so badly that the bull-fighting scene makes an annoying hole in the decorative schema and points up the unreality of this costume-piece instead of giving it the air of authenticity which it so sorely needs.

Manet, the reader must by now have gathered, was a fervent Hispanophil and, in this respect, typical of his period. *Hispagnolisme* – the fashion for things Spanish – had started with Romantic poets

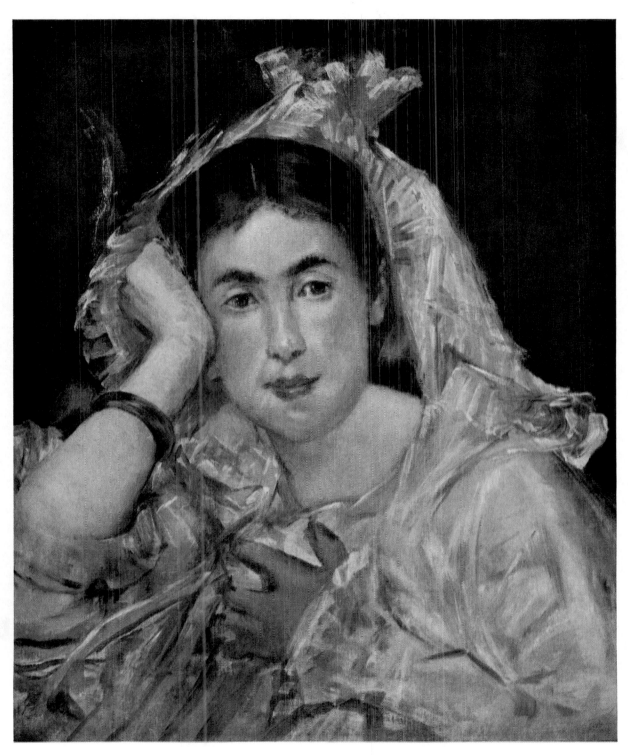

MARGUERITE DE CONFLANS WEARING A HOOD. 1873. Winterthur, Stiftung Dr. Oskar Reinhart

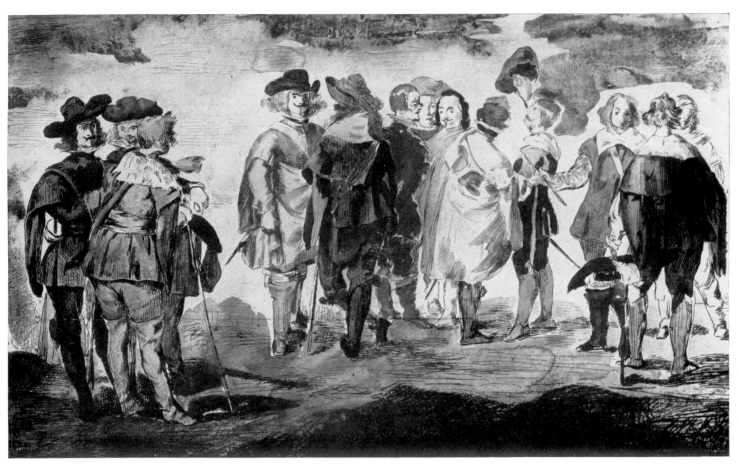

Fig. 1. A GROUP OF THIRTEEN CAVALIERS. Engraving heightened with watercolour. About 1860. Present whereabouts unknown

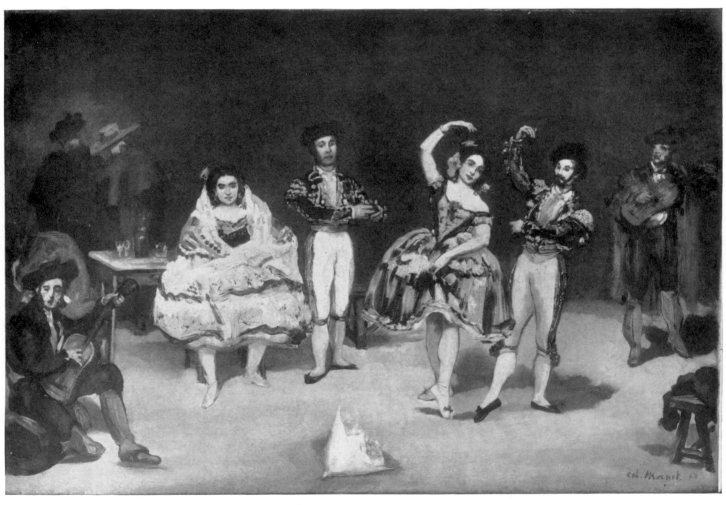

Fig 2. THE SPANISH DANCERS. Painting, 1862. Washington, Phillips Memorial Gallery

and writers like Gautier, Merimée and Hugo, and by the end of the 1830's had become a popular craze. By 1848, however, it was waning and might soon have died out if, in 1853, the Emperor had not married a Spanish beauty and thereby given it a new lease of life. Such facts as these are not irrelevant, for Manet was inordinately sensitive to fluctuations in fashion. But at the same time we must reckon with the possibility – or, to my mind, the probability – that Manet's *Hispagnolisme* also had its origins in a first-hand experience of Spanish art. Admittedly, this is denied by Baudelaire, but the poet is a far from reliable witness. It is extremely hard to believe that a precocious, gallery-going art-student like Manet did not make a point of visiting Marshal Soult's famous collection[2] of Spanish art before it was sold in 1852. That Manet was also familiar with the even more extensive collection of Spanish paintings formed by Louis-Philippe is likewise probable, since this was still on exhibition after Manet's 16th birthday. But even if he never actually saw either collection, he must have known most of what they contained at second-hand through the numerous engravings and copies that existed. Moreover, we must not forget that in 1853 and again in 1856 Manet travelled widely in order to familiarize himself with European art and, although he did not go to Spain, he did twice visit Vienna where the Hapsburg Velazquez' were on public exhibition.

The few works surviving from Manet's student days are mostly copies after the old masters, so we cannot be sure when the Spanish influence first manifested itself. Certain it is, however, that at the end of the 1850's, when the artist was breaking with Couture, he turned to Goya and Velazquez for help in the formation of his new style. Now it is not altogether a coincidence that Spanish mannerisms appear so frequently in Manet's art at this time, for in 1859 a series of Goya's engravings[3] was published which greatly impressed Baudelaire and his friends, Manet among them. Partly under the influence of these, Manet painted *Le Guitarrero* and a number of engravings in a Goyesque manner. I also suspect that the sharp contrasts of white and black, which he so much admired in Goya's graphic work, proved helpful to Manet in ridding his palette of half-tones. Velazquez was less easy to study in the Paris of 1860; nevertheless, Manet made paintings, drawings and engravings after various works then labelled Velazquez in the Louvre, notably the *Portrait of the Infanta Margareta* and *Les Petits Cavaliers*[4] (Fig. 1). At the same time he also painted two *Hommages à Velasquez*, imaginary scenes depicting the Spanish master and his models; and when in 1862 the Louvre purchased a *Portrait of Philip IV* Manet did a drawing and an engraving[5] after it.

Manet's style, as well as his subject-matter was deeply influenced by *Hispagnolisme*, especially by the various Spanish performers whom he saw at theatres and music halls in the early 1860's. The Andalusian guitarist, Huerta – one of the sensations of Paris in 1860 – undoubtedly gave Manet the idea for *Le Guitarrero*, just as Mariano Camprubi's troupe of dancers, who appeared in 1862, inspired a series of *genre* scenes, for which Victorine Meurent and the artist's brother posed, as well as a number of works

[2] Marshal Soult's collection, formed during the Peninsular War, included nearly 200 Spanish works, 20 by Zurbaran and 15 by Murillo. Louis-Philippe's collection, formed in Spain by Baron Taylor, comprised some 400 items, including 19 paintings attributed to Velazquez and 8 to Goya. Both these collections were enormously popular in the 1840's with French artists, some of whom banded themselves together into a group which became known as the *École Franco-Espagnole*.

[3] These were published by the Englishman Lumley who had bought up a number of the original copper plates. Manet was also a great admirer of Canaletto's engravings, as the curious linear shading in the background of many of his prints bears out.

[4] Tabarant and others claim that this copy was executed as early as 1855, but it is far more freely and confidently handled than *Le Buveur d'Absinthe* and would therefore seem to date from about 1860, the year when Manet is thought to have engraved the same subject. Formerly attributed to Velazquez, the original is now said to be by Mazo.

[5] Hitherto incorrectly dated. The Louvre *Philip IV* is now thought to be a studio copy by Mazo.

done from life (e.g. Plate 7 and Fig. 2). Likewise, when a *cartel* of bull-fighters arrived in Paris in 1863, Manet made a point of getting them to come to his studio. The result is *La Posada*, a group of toreadors in a tavern preparing for a bullfight. Once again, as in *Les Petits Cavaliers*, the figures – more than a dozen of them – are disposed in a frieze-like manner, and once again the composition does not altogether cohere, although this gives it a certain life-like awkwardness. Not so Manet's other tauromachic composition of this period, *L'Épisode d'une course de taureaux*. Abandoned and then reworked, this was ultimately shown at the Salon in 1864, but the critics were so unanimous in condemning the disproportion of its various parts (Edmond About compared the microscopic bull to a rat) that Manet cut out the two finest sections – the more important being *Torero Mort* (Plate 14), a close variant on the *Orlando Muerto*[6] (National Gallery, London) – and destroyed the rest of the composition. After this disappointment he painted no more Spanish subjects until he returned from Spain in 1865. But the Spanish masters continued to hold sway over his work.

Manet's *Hispagnolisme* has been examined at some length, because it was largely responsible for transforming him from a brilliant student into a mature and original artist. By soaking himself in the work of the Spanish masters, Manet learnt how to condense and simplify his pictorial effects, how to produce natural groupings and attitudes, how to use blacks and greys as active colours and how to apply paint in a rich, loose and liquid manner far removed from the dry and costive *touche* advocated by Couture. And by learning how to paint Spanish subjects from life without relying on picturesque, romantic or exotic effects, Manet developed the straightforward, detached approach of the 'Peintre de la vie moderne', a role in which he made some of his most impressive artistic contributions, in the early 1860's and particularly in the late 1870's.

When Baudelaire evolved the conception of the 'Peintre de la vie moderne' – the artist who would 'extract from fashion whatever poetry it might contain' and separate 'the eternal from the transitory' – he had Constantin Guys in mind. But his famous article applies just as well to Manet who was already a close friend of the poet's before 1860. Baudelaire defined 'the painter of modern life' as a dandy, a stroller who mixes with the crowd, watches the world go by, is in the midst of things and yet, as a personality, remains hidden. He envisaged a man with a natural curiosity about life who was anxious to appreciate everything going on around him, but content to stand on the periphery and remain impartial. Is this not precisely what Manet aspired to be? It is certainly an exact description of his attitude, when in 1862 he executed his first great scene of contemporary life, *La Musique aux Tuileries* (Plate 5) – a picture of prime importance for the development not only of Manet's *oeuvre* but of modern French art. True, *La Musique*, as has frequently been pointed out, is derivative in composition, for it recalls XVIIIth-century *études de moeurs* by Saint-Aubin and Debucourt and also has affinities with a lithograph by Daumier and with scenes of Parisian life by Guys[7] and other draughtsmen who worked for illustrated papers. But in every other respect it is original: it is the first out-of-doors scene (as opposed to a straightforward nature study) which is entirely convincing as such; it is the first important French painting to sacrifice 'finish' and 'detail' to the general impression of an animated scene; it is the first record of XIXth-century bourgeois life that is detached, realistic and seemingly spontaneous while yet being a work of art; indeed, it has quite a claim to be the first truly modern picture, at any

[6] This work, which has been variously attributed to Velazquez, Zurbaran and Karel Skreta, and now tentatively assigned to the Neapolitan School, was formerly in the Pourtalès collection, where Manet presumably saw it.

[7] Manet owned 60 drawings by Guys whom he knew well (through Baudelaire) and of whom he did a pastel portrait in 1879.

rate in Baudelaire's sense of the word 'modern'. Here we find none of the prettification or fashion-plate triviality which detract from comparable subjects by Isabey or Lami, nor – at the other extreme – the studio stuffiness or heavy-handed social comment which sometimes mar Courbet's realistic evocations of rural life. *La Musique* celebrates no particular incident. It is a literal record of everyday life, and it was this fact which provoked an uproar when it was exhibited. The 'slapdash' manner of its execution was bad enough, but what most irritated the Parisians was to see themselves depicted informally, as they really were.

For much the same reasons the public attacked Manet's other key-picture of 1862, *La Chanteuse des Rues* (Plate 6), which depicts a drab-looking Parisian street-singer emerging from a low tavern. Had there been a touch of pathos in the treatment of the subject, the public might have overlooked its ordinariness; after all Alfred Stevens' similar composition, *La Mendiante Tolérée*, had been well received in 1855, because, for all its realism, it told a story. But there is nothing sentimental or anecdotal about *La Chanteuse des Rues*; worse, as Paul Mantz pointed out, 'there is nothing more here than the shattering discord of chalky tones with black ones. The effect is pallid, harsh, ominous.' Manet's abandonment of half-tones was of course partly to blame for this 'shattering discord', but we must also consider another element which creeps into his style at this time: the influence of Japanese prints. Look, for instance, at the way the street-singer is reduced to a sort of bell-shaped cut-out, her dress being treated as an almost two-dimensional surface on which trimmings and folds form a bold, linear pattern, as in an Utamaro or a Hokusai. In *La Chanteuse* the *japonnerie* is still rudimentary, but in subsequent works – *Olympia* and *Le Fifre*, for example – it becomes a dominant stylistic ingredient. However, Manet always makes such discreet use of *japonnerie*, blending it with elements from Spanish and Venetian art and even from *images d'Épinal*, that one seldom realizes what an active role it plays. For instance, at first sight, the *Portrait de Zola* (Plate 24) seems to owe its conception to Venetian art; and yet, when closely studied, this canvas proves to be based on a decorative arrangement of flattened, vari-coloured forms such as one sees in the print by Utamaro in the background. Definite traces of Japanese influence are likewise to be found in the treatment of the negress and the setting of *Olympia*, of the right-hand figure in *Le Balcon* (Frontispiece), in *La Femme aux Éventails* (Louvre, Paris) and in many later pictures.

Manet was not the first XIXth-century painter, of course, to discover or to exploit the stylistic possibilities of Japanese art. On the contrary, *japonnerie* had been in fashion with a restricted *avant-garde* circle since the mid-1850's when Félix Bracquemond (the engraver), the Goncourts and, a little later, Baudelaire had started to popularise Japanese wood-engravings. When Manet was forming his style, *japonnerie*, like *Hispagnolisme*, was in the air. As early as 1858 Whistler, who is said to have been much impressed by some Hiroshige prints he had discovered in a tea shop near London Bridge, had painted *La Princesse du Pays de la Porcelaine*. But this early manifestation of *japonnerie* is perhaps of less significance than Whistler's subsequent exercises in an oriental manner, for in it he merely exploits the quaintly decorative, fancy-dress possibilities of the idiom. Manet, whose vision was far more profound and original than Whistler's, was attracted not by the trappings but by the essence of this unfamiliar art. And he used it, not to give an artificially spicy flavour to *genre* subjects, but as a key ingredient of the modern style which he was creating. Through studying Japanese prints, Manet learnt how to flatten his forms, how to simplify his spatial notation, how to dispense with a perspectival continuum, how to arrive at a rhythmic, linear structure and how to give his 'naïve' compositions a measure of decorative unity. Manet's imaginative exploitation of *japonnerie* is of the utmost importance for the subsequent development of XIXth-century art, for it revealed to Degas, the Impressionists and post-Impressionists (notably Gauguin, Toulouse-Lautrec and Van Gogh) a convenient escape route from the academic *impasse* in which European art was trapped.

Japonnerie and *Hispagnolisme* were not the only mid-century phenomena to influence Manet's style; the camera also plays an important role. Here again Manet gives evidence of his perception and originality. Most artists of the period, as Baudelaire complained, were trying to pit their puny resources against the new invention by attempting to produce pictures as accurate and detailed as photographs. On the other hand, Manet, himself an expert amateur photographer, realized that there was no call for the artist to sell out to Daguerre, because the camera obviated the need for excessive representationalism. Moreover he saw that he could learn a great deal from the way in which the impartial eye of the camera recorded things as they really were, and in sharp contrasts of black and white. Like Degas, Manet occasionally worked from photographs; one of his engraved portraits of Baudelaire, for instance, is based on a photograph by Nadar – a close friend of both artist and poet – in which candle light has been used to obtain a dramatic *chiaroscuro* effect. Manet may also have made some use of photographs when working on likenesses of various friends and celebrities in *La Musique*. Yet another interesting and hitherto unrecorded instance of Manet's use of the camera is provided by a drawing, *Le Printemps* (Fogg Art Museum) which has been traced over a faint photographic print of the original painting (Plate 33); this appears to be a unique case, though it might be unwise to assume that Manet never resorted to this process on other occasions. But the most significant, at the same time most elusive, manifestation of the camera's influence on Manet's vision is to be found in the frozen, naturalistic poses and 'dead-pan' expressions – so redolent of the photographer's studio – which are characteristic of virtually all his portraits and figure-paintings done before 1870: for example those of Victorine Meurent (Fig. 4 and Plates 6, 8 and 9), Léon Leenhoff (Plate 21) or Berthe Morisot (on the left in Frontispiece). What are these models staring at so intently, yet so vacantly? Not the artist, one feels, but Nadar's 'magic box'. And why this mask-like impassivity? Here Manet's Baudelairean cult of dandyism provides the answer. A dispassionate approach allowed Manet to capture 'the character of a dandy's beauty', which, according to Baudelaire, 'lies in the coldness of the gaze, the outward expression of an unshakeable resolution not to be moved. One could compare it to a dormant fire whose existence we can only guess at, for it refuses to burst into flame. This (Baudelaire was actually referring to Guys, but these words are more applicable to Manet) is what these pictures express to perfection.'

By the end of 1862 Manet had every reason to feel satisfied: in one year he had completed over a dozen major and numerous minor works, had managed to transform his hesitant manner into a strong, supple and personal style and, no less important, had discovered how to express on canvas the life of his native city and of his own time. Not unnaturally he was eager to exhibit what he had done as soon as possible, so as to prove that he was no longer a promising beginner; consequently fourteen of his best paintings were put on show at the Galerie Martinet at the beginning of March 1863. Manet hoped that they would enjoy such popular success that the Salon jurors would unhesitatingly accept three others which he proposed to submit to them later in the spring. But his optimism was as usual misplaced and his one-man show – an innovation to which the public was not as yet accustomed – was received with vituperative abuse by all but a minority of critics and a few young painters (Monet and Bazille among them). One visitor even threatened to attack *La Musique* with his walking stick.

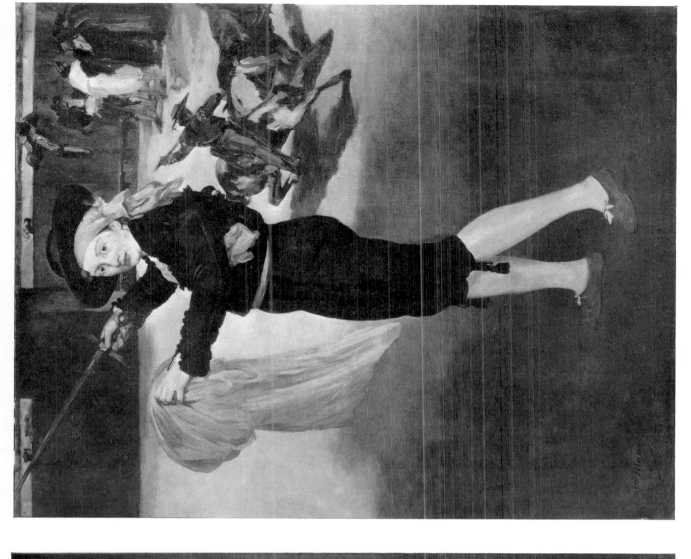

Fig. 4. MLLE. VICTORINE IN THE COSTUME OF AN ESPADA. Painting. 1862.
New York, Metropolitan Museum

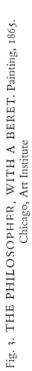

Fig. 3. THE PHILOSOPHER, WITH A BERET. Painting, 1865.
Chicago, Art Institute

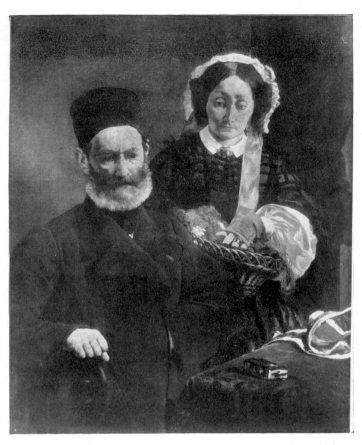

Fig. 5. PORTRAIT OF MONSIEUR AND MADAME
AUGUSTE MANET. Painting, 1860.
Paris, Private Collection

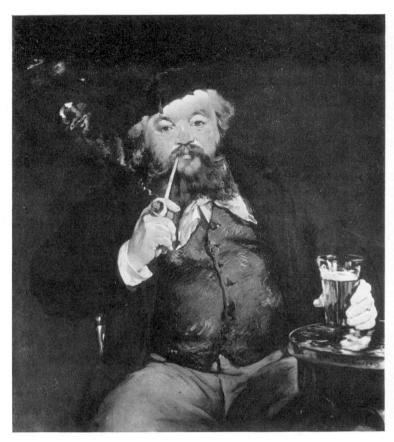

Fig. 6. LE BON BOCK. Painting, 1873. Philadelphia Museum of Art
(Mr. and Mrs. Carroll S. Tyson Jr. Collection)

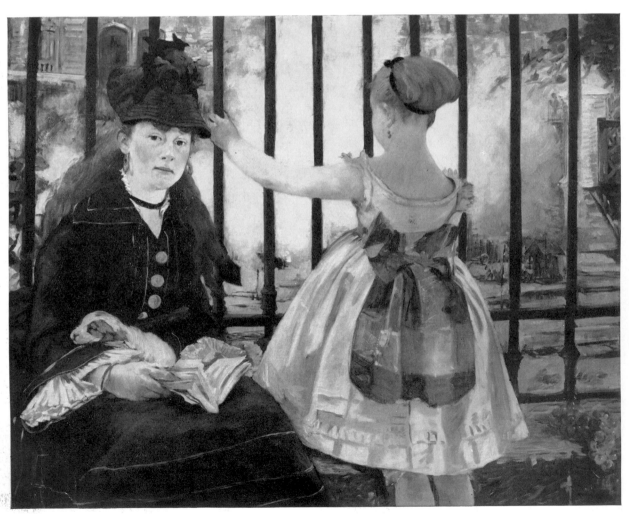

Fig. 7. THE RAILWAY. Painting, 1873. Washington, National Gallery of Art (Gift of Horace Havemeyer)

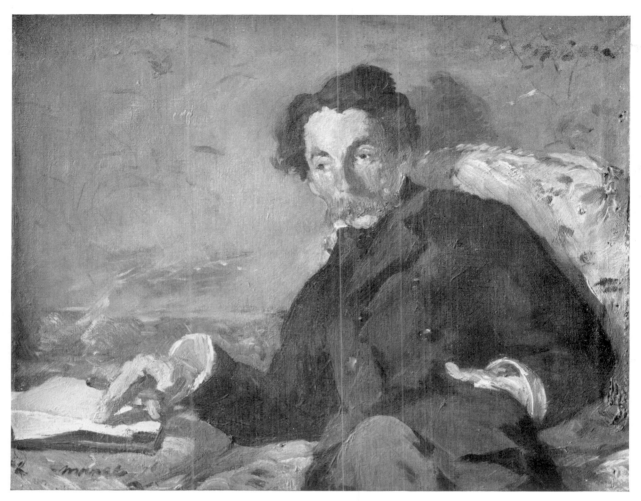

Fig. 8. PORTRAIT OF STÉPHANE MALLARMÉ. Painting, 1876. Paris, Louvre

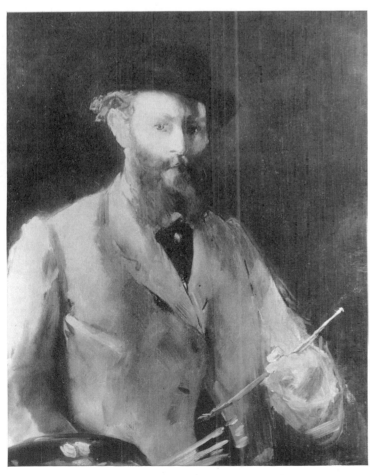

Fig. 9. SELF-PORTRAIT WITH PALETTE. Painting,
1879. New York, John L. Loeb Collection

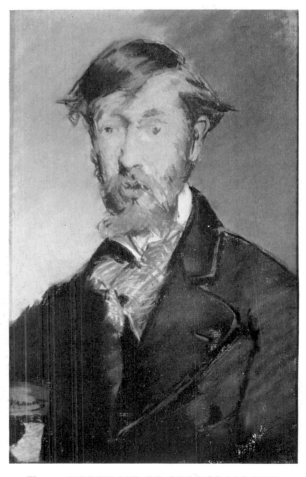

Fig. 10. PORTRAIT OF GEORGE MOORE.
Pastel, 1879. New York, Metropolitan Museum

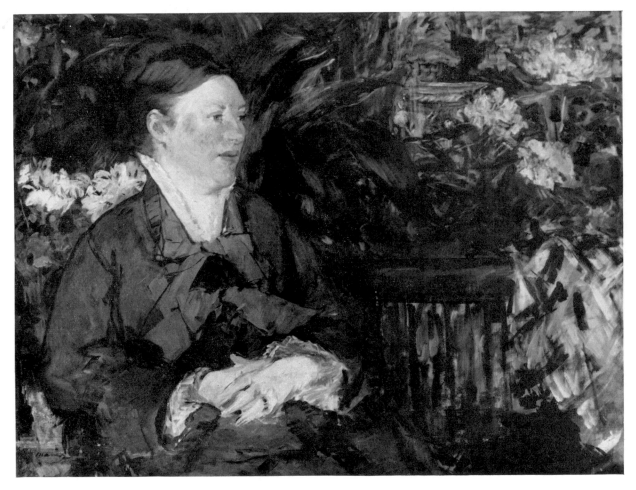

Fig. 11. MADAME ÉDOUARD MANET IN THE CONSERVATORY. Painting, 1879.
Oslo, National Gallery

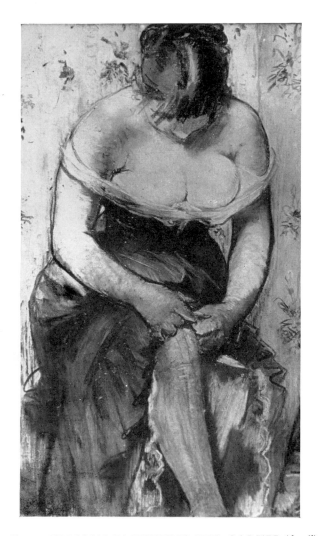

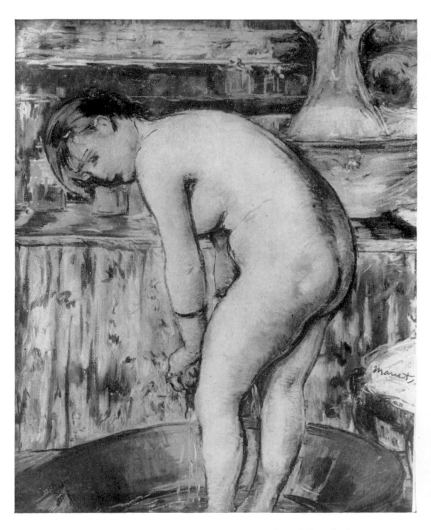

Fig. 12. WOMAN FASTENING HER GARTER (detail).
Pastel, about 1878. Ordrupsgaard, Wilhelm Hansen Museum

Fig. 13. WOMAN WASHING HERSELF. Pastel, about
1878. Paris, Bernheim-Jeune Collection

Worse was to come; Manet's three Salon entries – *Jeune Homme en costume de majo, Mlle Victorine en costume d'espada* (Fig. 4) and *Le Déjeuner sur l'herbe* (Plate 8) – were rejected. With good reason Manet protested; nor was he the only artist to do so. More than 4,000 works were refused by the Salon jury that year, including paintings by Cézanne, Whistler, Pissarro, Fantin-Latour and Jongkind, and the ensuing complaints were so loud and numerous that the Emperor was forced to take notice of them. More out of a desire to prove the Salon jury right than out of any desire to display his own liberal feelings, the Emperor decreed that all the rejected pictures should be exhibited together in the Palais de l'Industrie. Manet, who seldom despaired for long, welcomed this opportunity of displaying his work, but once again his hopes were to be shattered. The public and critics (except for Zacharie Astruc and Thoré-Bürger) were in no mood to be lenient to the *Salon des Refusés*, as the Exhibition came to be known; and while they jeered at everything, they singled out Manet's work, especially *Le Déjeuner sur l'herbe*, for their scorn. Manet's name thus became a household joke, and from this time virtually until the end of his life he was consistently attacked or dismissed by the majority of critics, while the few who genuinely admired his work – such as Théodore Duret – could not always be sure that their notices would be printed.

Little is to be gained by quoting at length from the journalistic attacks on Manet beyond the insight which they afford into the depths of Second Empire philistinism. For Manet's persecutors were on the whole ill-informed and obtuse, and their invective casts darkness rather than light on his achievements. So far as one can see, what most shocked people about *Le Déjeuner sur l'herbe* was that it treated a *risqué* subject seriously. Had Manet presented his picnic as a titilating *scène galante*, had he treated it in an idyllic or pastoral instead of a modern manner, or had he dressed up the men in doublet and hose and given his composition a high-falutin' poetic title, the public might have been less incensed. What they could not stomach was the naturalism of the conception, the absence of anecdotal detail and sentiment, and the fact that light, instead of being conventionally golden, is clear, cool and shines equally on the whole scene instead of being artfully used to pick out pretty passages. Moreover, as every artist knew, it was only permissible to dispense with half-tones when representing the Godhead. Manet's solecism was to extend this treatment to a 'commonplace woman of the *demi-monde*, as naked as can be, shamelessly lolling between two dandies dressed to the teeth'.

Had Manet really been (as Paul Colin and others have maintained) a cowardly traditionalist, he would presumably have heeded his critics and adjusted his style. But much as he longed for recognition and popularity at this time, Manet made no concessions to bourgeois taste and continued in a more, rather than a less, revolutionary way. After finishing *Le Déjeuner sur l'herbe*, he embarked on *Olympia* (Plates 9 and 11), the work which the artist always considered as his masterpiece. And rightly so, for it is a triumphant proof of the power and originality of the style which Manet had arrived at by a laborious process of synthesis, a style which anticipates much of the best XXth-century art in being based on conceptual rather than perceptual elements. *Olympia* is a tremendous advance on *Le Déjeuner sur l'herbe* painted only a few months before. Forms are more ruthlessly flattened and simplified and the main *motif* of the picture – the figure, the bed, the bouquet and the maid (or rather her dress) – is restricted to a lightly modelled, lightly coloured mass silhouetted against a dark background. And yet, despite its seeming flatness, *Olympia* evokes a sensation of volume, thanks to a few cunningly placed shadows, to the subtle suggestion of an outline (one of Manet's most criticized innovations, and yet what could be more orthodoxly classical?) and to the heavy impasto of cream-coloured paint, which gives to the girl's body a marvellous tactile quality and fleshy density. *Olympia* has become so hackneyed that its beauties are difficult to appreciate today but, to my mind, no amount of reproductions can stale its radiance or its freshness.

What did Manet think would happen when he exhibited *Olympia* at the Salon of 1865? Admittedly he was somewhat naïve, but still he cannot have been so naïve as to imagine that the style and subject of his latest picture were anything other than provocative. Indeed, one may well ask why, if he was not out to provoke, he should have inscribed on the frame the first verse of a poem in which Olympia is addressed as 'l'auguste jeune fille'. Once again, the answer lies partly in the innate duality of Manet's character and partly in his Baudelairean cult of dandyism, in his enjoyment of 'the pleasure of astounding people combined with the arrogant satisfaction of never being astounded oneself'. For while Manet wanted to astonish people, he also hoped that *Olympia* would find admirers. Optimistic as ever, he seems to have believed that the Salon public had expended its rage in the previous year and would therefore be inured to the novelty of his conception. There was even a possibility that they might applaud him for giving fresh dignity to a *genre* which had been degraded by the followers of Ingres. The situation was ironical, for the Parisian gallery-goers – who, Zola complained, had bullied a generation of over-indulgent painters into pandering to their least whim – were under a similar delusion: according to Duret, they were convinced that Manet, knowing their feelings, would make allowances and modify his style. Naturally, when the Salon opened, both sides were disenchanted. The public, and the critics who voiced public opinion, revenged themselves by hounding Manet as few artists have been hounded before or since. 'A yellow-bellied courtesan', *Olympia* was called, 'a female gorilla made of india-rubber outlined in black'. Even Courbet, hitherto a partisan of Manet's, is said to have compared her to 'the Queen of Spades after her bath'. When words failed, physical attacks were made on the picture, which was only saved by being hung out of reach above a door in the last gallery, 'where you scarcely knew whether you were looking at a parcel of nude flesh or a bundle of laundry'. Nevertheless, as Paul de Saint-Victor wrote, the mob continued 'to crowd round Manet's gamey *Olympia* and disgusting *Ecce Homo* as if they were at the morgue'.

As with *Le Déjeuner sur l'herbe*, it was not only the stylistic innovations of *Olympia* which infuriated people, but the 'shamelessness', 'immorality' and 'vulgarity' of the subject. Here was a naked girl, whom anybody could recognize (one of the few nudes in art of which this can be said), not an anonymous nude masquerading as a Circassian slave, coquettish Bathsheba, simpering nymph or frigid, ideal beauty. *Olympia* reclines – appropriately enough – on a bed and receives from her black maid a bouquet, a tribute to her charms. Now the Salon public was partial to *risqué* subjects – Clésinger's sculpture, *Femme piquée par un serpent* (1847), which in reality depicts a woman in the throes of orgasm, caused something of a scandal but was far more enthusiastically received than *Olympia* – so long as the real action was disguised by some polite convention, that is to say dressed up as allegory – e.g. Couture's *Courtisane Moderne* (Museum of Fine Arts, Philadelphia) – or presented as a castigation of sin. Manet, however, was too much of a dandy to dissemble or moralize, and his *demi-mondaine* is portrayed with characteristic detachment – naked, unabashed (the critics of course said 'brazen') and unmistakably a Parisienne of her time; just the sort of Parisienne, indeed, that many a Salon visitor kept hidden from his wife. All this so scandalized people that by the time the Salon closed Manet's notoriety, said Degas, had become 'as great as Garibaldi's'; in fact, it had attained such proportions that instead of 'enjoying the arrogant satisfaction of not being astonished', Manet discovered that he had become the unenviable butt of public ridicule. At this point he lost confidence and found himself unable to go on painting. From Brussels, Baudelaire wrote to console and also to upbraid him for his un-dandyish despair: 'Do you think that you are the first man to find himself in this plight? Are you more of a genius than Chateaubriand or Wagner? After all everybody made fun of them and it did not kill them.' But 'the apostle of the ugly and repulsive', as Manet had been called, refused to be comforted and, in order to escape his persecutors, fled to Spain.

Before discussing the consequences of the artist's visit to Spain, I should like to digress for a moment and comment on the accusations of plagiarism which are constantly being levelled at Manet. Jacques-Emile Blanche, for instance, is supposed to have said that 'there existed virtually no painting of consequence by Manet that was not inspired by another picture either ancient or modern'; while Christian Zervos has written that Manet 'borrowed the eyes and feelings of artists of the past to such an extent that a real sensation does not exist in his work'. Now this last statement was made not gratuitously, but apropos the centenary exhibition of Manet's work held in Paris in 1932, on which occasion certain French art-historians were prompted to accuse Manet of having pilfered ideas from masters[8] of every school and period and to track down precedents – not always convincing – for most of his important compositions. The unfortunate painter was thus saddled with a thoroughly confusing artistic lineage, and Michel Florisoone, for example, put forward the theory that Manet's *Hispagnolisme* 'was far less personal than his *Vénétianisme*'. Of course Manet admired the Venetians – what great French artist of his time did not? – and his works include recognizable quotations from Venetian paintings. But it is surely going much too far to claim, as Florisoone does, that the compositions of *La Lecture* (Plate 20), *Le Chemin de fer* (Fig. 7), *Chez le Père Lathuille* (Plate 40) and 'all the half-length portraits in a rectangle' were inspired by Titian's *Allegory of Alfonso d'Avalos* (Louvre). As it happens, *La Lecture* bears a much closer resemblance to Goya's *Portrait of Godoy* (Prado), which Manet presumably knew, and *Chez le Père Lathuille* could equally well be based on the composition of Boucher's *Cage* (Louvre). Is it not just as likely, on the other hand, that these correspondences are coincidental? Manet was after all a spontaneous and intuitive artist out to capture the naturalistic poses of real life; might he not have stumbled by chance on a composition which had been used before? His *Joueuse de Guitare* (Tabarant No. 116) is very like a figure in Cariani's *Woman playing a lute and Shepherd asleep* (Bergamo), but we are not entitled to conclude from this that a new source has been identified, for Manet may well not have known this picture.

Let us look at the problem from another angle. Even if it could be proved that most of Manet's compositions derive from other masters, would this necessarily be in his disfavour? Was not Manet's 'crime' normal artistic practice in the XVIth, XVIIth and XVIIIth centuries? For example *The Venus of Urbino*, from which *Olympia* stems, is a variation on Giorgione's Dresden *Venus*, yet this has never militated against the originality of Titian, any more than the fact that Gauguin's *Woman with the Mangoes* (Moscow) is a variant on *Olympia* – in other words a variant on a variant of a variant – has militated against the originality of Gauguin. So long as the artist has sufficient vitality and artistry to transform his borrowings into something completely personal, does it matter where he finds his

[8] Manet is known to have copied works by Andrea del Sarto, Fra Angelico, Ghirlandajo, Filippino Lippi, Titian, Rembrandt, Brouwer, Velazquez, Mazo, Gérard and Delacroix among others. On various occasions he has been said to have been influenced by Mantegna, Giorgione, Raphael, Titian, Tintoretto, Veronese, Caravaggio, the Carracci, Canaletto (the engravings), Rubens, Hals, Rembrandt, Dutch *genre* painters, Greco, Murillo, Velazquez, Ribera, Goya, Watteau, Fragonard, Chardin, Boucher, Quentin de la Tour, Perronneau, David, Géricault, Couture, Delacroix, Constable and Bonington, as well as by XVIIIth-century *études de moeurs*, *images d'Epinal*, Japanese prints and English sporting-prints. Some of these influences are unquestionably identifiable in Manet's work; many, however, are not.

inspiration? Manet of course had these qualities; moreover, except in a few isolated instances, his original stimulus did not spring from the art of the past but from a real-life experience. Thus, instead of being *pastiches*, his paintings have a reality and organic life of their own. Take *Le Déjeuner sur l'herbe*: this was inspired by some bathers whom the artist saw at Argenteuil (*see* Note on Plate 8), but the bathers suggested the Giorgionesque treatment and Raphaelesque composition. The same is true of *Le Balcon* (*see* Note on Frontispiece), whose starting-point was not the painting by Goya, but the spectacle of a group of people on a balcony at Boulogne; the memory of Goya came later. The same pattern repeats itself for other compositions, but in each case the dissimilarities are more interesting than the similarities. Therefore, instead of dismissing Manet as an unimaginative plagiarist totally dependent on the art of the past, I feel that we should try to see him as an original and creative artist who arrived at his pictorial formulae, just as he arrived at his stylistic synthesis, by exploiting a Janus-like disposition and blending old and new elements in a new way.

Manet's visit to Spain was both a revelation and a disappointment: a revelation because the Spanish masters exceeded his highest hopes and the spectacle of Spanish life delighted him; a disappointment because the dirt and bad food revolted this most fastidious of men. Had Manet been in a less discouraged state, curiosity might have triumphed over disgust. As it was, he did not stay longer than ten days in Madrid – enough time to develop a taste for bull-fighting and to discover that, while Goya did not live up to his expectations, Velazquez was 'the painter of painters'. 'The most extraordinary work of this splendid *oeuvre* (Manet wrote to Fantin-Latour) and perhaps the most astonishing painting ever done is the *Portrait of a Celebrated Actor of the time of Philip IV*.[9] The background disappears; the life-like figure dressed in black is surrounded by nothing but air ... And what magnificent portraits! By contrast, Titian's *Charles V* seems made of wood.'

The outcome of this first-hand experience of Velazquez' work was a second phase of intense *Hispagnolisme*. The figure of *L'Acteur tragique* (Coll. Vanderbilt, New York), which Manet painted after[10] his return to Paris, is strongly reminiscent of the *Pablillos* and is steeped in the same airy, greyish element; while the two *Philosophers* (see Fig. 3) and a *Rag-and-bone-man* (with Wildenstein, New York) – large, full-length character studies of old men against plain, darkish backgrounds – are directly inspired by Velazquez' *Aesop* and *Menippus* (both Prado). Indeed, it is difficult not to feel that these interpretations of Velazquez are almost too literal; even their qualities – impressive old-masterish ones – remind us that they are among the few works by Manet which derive not from real life but from art. However, not all the paintings inspired by Manet's Spanish visit were so unoriginal. Three magnificent bull-fighting scenes, started in October 1865,[11] are entirely free of Velazquez' influence, being detached and naturalistic records, not vehicles for stylistic experiment, like so many other works of this phase. True, Manet has refreshed his memory by looking at Goya's *Tauromaquia* as well as at his own notes made in Madrid, but the vividness of these paintings bears out their origins in visual experience;

[9] Now known as *Pablillos of Valladolid* (Prado). Jamot-Wildenstein publish a copy (No. 116) of this work which Manet is said to have done in Spain. Tabarant, however, justifiably maintains that this is by another hand. A recently published watercolour (Kurt Martin: *Édouard Manet, Aquarelle und Pastelle*, Basel, 1958, Plate VIII) of a bull-fighting scene, also said to have been executed in Spain, is likewise not by Manet.

[10] On stylistic grounds, this could not have been painted before Manet went to Spain, as Tabarant claims.

[11] Tabarant assigns this group to 1866, but in a letter to Duret of October 1865 Manet says that he has already finished one bull-fighting scene.

and their naturalistic, seemingly casual compositions are much more satisfactory than those which Manet would have used before his Spanish journeys. While working on the bull-fighting scenes, Manet also returned to his stylistic pre-occupations in an engraving, *Au Prado*, showing two girls in mantillas being ogled by two *majos*. Stylistically this is particularly instructive, for if we compare its four successive states we can see how Manet, with the help of elements taken from Japanese art, transforms a naturalistic scene in the manner of Goya into a bold, flat pattern of simplified rhythmic shapes, such as one finds later in the work of Toulouse-Lautrec.

Much the same stylistic process can be followed if we compare the two works which Manet submitted, without success, to the Salon of 1866: *L'Acteur tragique*, painted in the autumn of 1865, and *Le Fifre* (Plate 19) of about six months later. Both paintings derive from Velazquez' *Pablillos*, in that both show figures 'surrounded by nothing but air'. But whereas the former only just escapes being pastiche, *Le Fifre* is a triumphantly original and daring synthesis of Spanish and Japanese elements – an advance even on *Olympia*. From Velazquez Manet has learnt how to conjure up an illusion of space out of an unrelieved expanse[12] of grey paint and a slight shadow (behind the right foot), while from the Japanese he has learnt how to arrive at a simple, but expressive and harmonious arrangement of flattish forms. Among Manet's contemporaries, Zola was almost alone in seeing what the artist was aiming at: 'One of our great modern landscape-painters,' he wrote, 'has said that this painting resembles an outfitter's signboard; I agree with him if he means by this that the boy's uniform has been treated with the simplicity of a popular print. The yellow of the braid, the blue-black of the tunic and the red of the trousers are just flat patches of colour. The simplification produced by the acute and perceptive eye of the artist has resulted in a canvas, all lightness and *naïveté*, charming to the point of elegance, yet realistic to the point of ruggedness.'

The harmony, clarity, economy and concentration on essentials which we find in *Le Fifre* are features of all Manet's best paintings, but more particularly of those done before 1869. Take, for instance, *L'Exécution de Maximilien* (Plate 17): how complex the incident Manet has chosen to depict, how concise the configuration! Yet the story is told dramatically, without rhetoric but with considerable pictorial effect. Likewise *Le Déjeuner dans l'atelier* (Plate 21) of the following year; this is one of Manet's most complex compositions, but it is rendered with such simplicity (the cat, for instance, is reduced to a sort of black hieroglyph) that it appears wonderfully fresh and life-like. By contrast, a much later work like *Dans la serre* (Berlin), although simple in composition, looks overloaded with detail and fussily painted.

One might think that such an intrinsically attractive work as *Le Déieuner* would have found favour with the critics and public, but in fact each new work by Manet which they saw incited them to mockery or rage. No wonder the artist's morale began to weaken! In the face of the fiasco of his one-man show in 1867, repeated rejections by the Salon jury and vituperative attacks in the press, Manet, who had hitherto alternated between extremes of optimism and pessimism, lapsed into a state of self-doubt and gloom. He virtually abandoned the stylistic synthesis which he had but recently perfected, painted less, destroyed an increasing quantity of works while still unfinished (Tabarant lists a mere six paintings done in 1867, and only seven in 1868), and no longer dared ask anyone outside his family and intimate circle of friends to pose for him.

---

[12] Courbet had already had recourse to a similar device in his *Portrait de Max Buchon* (Musée de Vevey) of about 1860, which Manet may conceivably have known. But the background of the Courbet has none of the luminosity or spatial depth of the Manet.

At this critical juncture in his artistic development, Manet had only one consolation: a group of young admirers – Monet, Bazille, Renoir and Berthe Morisot – who hailed him as a great originator. He was friendly with all of them, but especially with Berthe Morisot. A product of the *haute bourgeoisie* like Manet himself, this intelligent and striking-looking girl appealed to him because she was an obliging model with dramatic, rather Spanish features and a habit of dressing in his favourite combination of black and white – as witness some of Manet's most hallucinating portraits. But because she was also a modern artist with a style of her own, she was in a position to teach Manet something as well as to learn from him. Amateurish and slapdash her work sometimes is, but her amateurishness was apt to be touched with genius. We must also not forget that she was a great-great niece of Fragonard, as well as an ex-pupil of Corot: hence her freshness of vision and lightness of touch, qualities which significantly appear in Manet's paintings in 1869. Berthe Morisot was not of course the sole cause of Manet's change of idiom at the end of the 1860's – Monet, an infinitely more inventive artist, was also partly responsible – but I suspect that it was she who persuaded Manet to look at nature with a fresh eye and who was responsible for discouraging his obsession with stylistic considerations. The *Vue de l'Exposition Universelle* (National Gallery, Oslo) was inspired by one of Morisot's paintings; however, the Morisot-like tendency to softness, sketchiness and looseness in Manet's work does not fully emerge until the Boulogne pictures of 1869 and the landscape sketches done at Arcachon in 1871. Some of these might almost have been painted by Berthe Morisot; they are certainly not very good. All things considered, it is hard to feel that the inspired amateurishness and proto-Impressionist approach of his Egeria had an altogether improving effect on Manet's art, for with one or two notable exceptions (e.g. Plate 27 and the magnificent portraits of Berthe Morisot), the paintings of 1870–71 are sketchy and disturbingly eclectic in style. Had Manet been in better health or spirits, possibly his work would have been more vigorous and consistent, but the Siege of Paris, the Commune and the hysteria of post-war Paris life had left him in a wretchedly neurotic state. And the few paintings that date from this period of doubt and unrest reveal the artist wavering and seeking inspiration alternately in the works of Berthe Morisot, Goya and Monet, reverting briefly to his own 'flat' style of the mid-1860's, then finally, after a visit to Holland in the summer of 1872, launching into a Dutch style *genre-piece*, *Le Bon Bock* (Fig. 6).

Le Bon Bock is unique in Manet's *oeuvre*. It is more worked on than most,[13] represents a deliberate attempt 'to make the critics swallow their words' – an attempt, it must be said, which succeeded, for when the picture was exhibited at the Salon of 1873[14] it was warmly praised – and lastly reveals the extent of Manet's temporary infatuation with the work of Hals[15] and the Dutch *genre* painters. On the strength of this untypical and in many ways unpleasing work, Manet has been represented as a XIXth-century reincarnation of Hals. This view too is erroneous, for most of Manet's supposedly Hals-like mannerisms stem from Velazquez and make their appearance in his work well before the visit to Haarlem in 1872 (e.g. *Le Jeune Homme à la Poire* of 1869; National Museum, Stockholm). And it is a curious fact that, with occasional exceptions (e.g. text Plate), Manet's most Hals-like paintings of the 1870's usually turn out to be unfinished works. Not that there is anything significant or mysterious

[13] The model, a lithographer called Émile Bellot, had to endure 80 sittings.

[14] Significantly Manet's other Salon Offering, *Le Repos* – a much finer work (Coll. Vanderbilt, New York) – was universally condemned. 'The Goddess of slovenliness', 'Seasickness', 'A lady resting after having swept the chimney' are some of the epithets applied to it by the critics.

[15] 'He is drinking Haarlem beer' was Alfred Stevens' malicious comment on *Le Bon Bock* – a comment which so infuriated Manet that he gave up seeing his old friend for some time.

about this; the explanation is simply that Manet blocked in his compositions with broad, hatched brush-strokes which bear a quite fortuitous resemblance to the *facture* of Hals.

Stylistic and aesthetic considerations apart, *Le Bon Bock* is important in that it marks the end of a difficult period. Encouraged by having at last had a success at the Salon, by the fact that Durand-Ruel had recently bought a number of his paintings and, not least, by the gaiety which had returned to Paris with the Third Republic, Manet resumed painting scenes which would express some of the more agreeable aspects of the life of his time. Outstanding among these are *Le Chemin de fer* (Fig. 7) and *Le Bal masqué à l'Opéra* (Coll. Havemeyer, New York), a delightfully life-like *scène de moeurs* similar in composition and spirit to *La Musique aux Tuileries*. At the same time Manet found himself drifting more than ever into the orbit of the Impressionists. Here, however, we must tread carefully, for Manet's flirtation with members of this movement has been the cause of misunderstandings ever since the group was first dubbed '*la bande à Manet*' in the 1870's. Manet's stylistic discoveries, his rejection of a high academic finish, his use of pure colour and his naturalistic view of life had set an example which decisively influenced the Impressionists. But they owed him no allegiance and over many fundamental problems, regarding the representation of light and optical reactions to colour, his views and theirs were diametrically opposed. The Impressionists were never in any real sense a '*bande à Manet*'; nor, as is so often claimed, was Manet in any real sense one of them, and certainly not, as Roger Fry wrote, 'a great painter for whom Impressionism was an aberration'. Manet never painted a truly Impressionist picture, that is to say one in which no black is used and colour is broken up into its complementaries, largely because he never visualized a scene purely in terms of light. For these reasons Manet always refused to exhibit with the Impressionists, preferring, as he said, to stand or fall on his own at the Salon. Manet was only an Impressionist to the limited extent that, under the aegis of Monet and to a lesser degree of Renoir,[16] he took to using a lighter palette, painting in stippled and broken brush-strokes and experimenting more often than before with open-air subjects (e.g. Plates 29 and 31). Far from harming Manet's art, the Impressionist influence had a most beneficial effect; his finest compositions of the mid-1870's – *Argenteuil* (Plate 23), for instance – are more homogeneous in handling, richer and more varied in *facture* and more brilliant in tone than those of the previous decade. Defects there are in some of Manet's work of the period – a falling-off in intensity and a tendency to indulge in *belle peinture* for its own sake – but these have nothing to do with Impressionism. On the contrary, they stem partly from ill-health, partly from discouragement in the face of the intransigently hostile attitude of the critics, Salon jury and public[17] and partly, one suspects, from Manet's growing friendship with the poet Mallarmé who seems to have encouraged the artist's latent aestheticism, his Elstir-like tendency[18] to cultivate the exquisite.

[16] The oft-repeated story, originally recounted by Vollard, that Manet had a low opinion of Renoir's work is persuasively claimed by Tabarant to be a misunderstanding or an invention.

[17] The success of *Le Bon Bock* was not repeated. Of Manet's four Salon entries in 1874, two were rejected and two violently attacked by the critics; in 1875 his one exhibit, *Argenteuil*, was mercilessly criticized; in 1876 his two entries were rejected ('Reject him! Let's reject him! Let him stay by himself with his two paintings', cried the jurors); in 1877 *Nana* was rejected and the *Portrait de Faure* accepted, but Cham published a caricature entitled 'Hamlet gone mad has had himself painted by Manet'; in 1878 he was too discouraged to send anything in; in 1879 and 1880 Manet exhibited two works, but the critics were mostly luke-warm, and it was not until 1880 that the artist was awarded the Salon medal which he had always coveted and which entitled him to exhibit what he liked at future Salons.

[18] The imaginary painter, Elstir, in Proust's *Remembrance of Things Past* has much in common with Manet.

By 1877–78 Manet and the Impressionists had drifted, artistically speaking, apart. Manet reverted to doing *plein-air* scenes during the last two years of his life, it is true, but all his really great late works depict not nature but mankind, and the female of the species in particular. Now it is interesting that Manet should once have said that he never painted the quintessential woman of the Second Empire, but only of the Third Republic – interesting because at the very beginning of his career Manet already prided himself on being a 'painter of modern life'. Perhaps Manet would have painted life under the Second Empire more fully if he had felt less antipathy for the vulgar ostentation and totalitarianism of the epoch. As it is, *La Chanteuse des rues* and *Olympia*, while being very much of their period, are more important for the stylistic innovations they represent than for the light they throw on their time. However, Manet's paintings of women of the 1870's are fascinating and evocative images of a period, whereas stylistically they are of comparatively little interest.

We have only to compare Manet with Degas to appreciate that whereas Degas shows us different aspects of an anonymous female animal – *l'éternel féminin* – Manet in his later works shows us the changing face of the Parisenne of the Third Republic – variously a courtesan, *grande dame*, actress, barmaid, bourgeoise, intellectual spinster and street-girl. What is more, he has taken care to see that the costume, coiffure and pose are appropriate to the sitter and typical of the time.

A chonicler of fashion? Yes, but also a chronicler of life. That is perhaps Manet's greatest quality. In his magnificent series of *genre* scenes of 1877 onwards – *La Prune* (Plate 36), *Le Skating* (Wertheim Collection, New York, on jacket), *Au Café* (Plate 39) and *Le Bar* (Plates 45 and 47), for example – one feels that Manet has somehow managed to stop the clock, for each of these works pins down for ever a moment of time in terms of great art. This is what distinguishes Manet from the lesser lights of his day – men like Tissot, Béraud and Stevens – who also set out to portray the passing show; this and the fact that Manet retained to the end his dispassionate and naturalistic vision. He always managed to see his period in perspective, whereas others made the mistake of handling fashionable subjects in an academic or modish way, with the consequence that their works – once so *chic* and up-to-the-minute – now seem at best quaint or 'amusing', at worst as lifeless as an old fashion-plate.

Manet's illness and premature death in 1883 were a much more serious blow for modern art than is generally realized. For, by the end of the 1870's, Manet had begun to take all kinds of daring pictorial liberties; had learnt how to obtain richer and more varied effects; had developed a more striking sense of colour; had considerably widened his imaginative range and had overcome his compositional failings. He himself seems to have felt that he was far from having nothing more to say, that, on the contrary, his best years lay ahead. And what more likely? The Salon public was finally coming to tolerate his novel style and vision, and it is more than probable that popular success would have spurred him on to excel himself. *Le Bar*, his culminant work, opens up tantalizing vistas of unpainted masterpieces, of a series of stupendous allegorical scenes of modern life which he envisaged.

Alas, instead of going on to paint more and more ambitious pictures, Manet was condemned by illness to work on an increasingly restricted scale – hence the impressionistic garden-scenes, the pastel portraits and flowerpieces of 1880 to 83 – until in the last year of his life he seriously considered taking up miniature painting. This was Manet's tragedy – a more bitter tragedy, to my mind, than the blindness of Monet and Degas, more bitter even than the early deaths of Seurat and Toulouse-Lautrec, because each of these artists had been able to create an *oeuvre* that is homogeneous and complete. Manet was a great originator, a great executant, a great artist and a great influence; nevertheless the *oeuvre* which he left behind is, in the last resort, incomplete and only partly fulfilled.

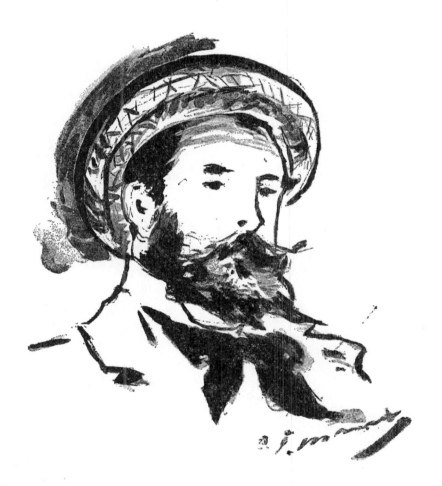

PLATES

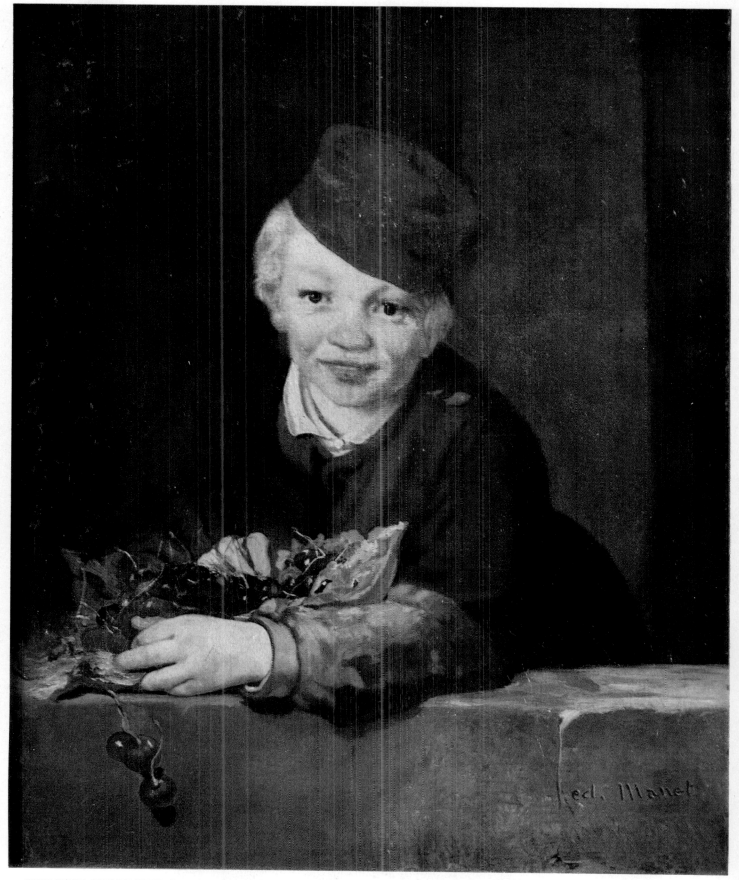

1. THE BOY WITH THE CHERRIES. 1858–60. Lisbon, Gulbenkian Foundation

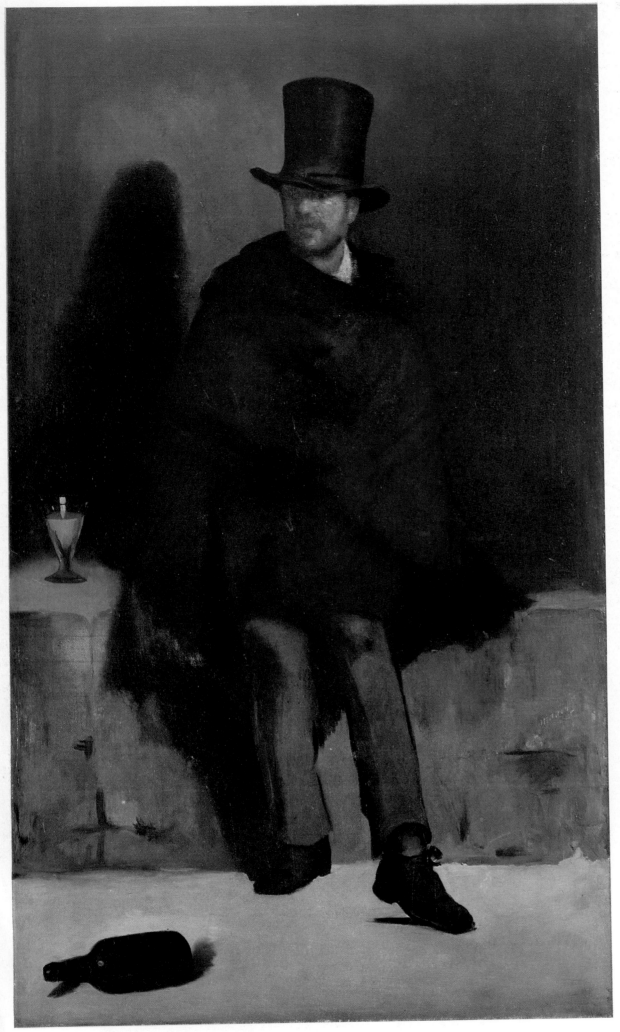

2. THE ABSINTHE-DRINKER. 1858–9. Copenhagen, Ny Carlsberg Glyptotek

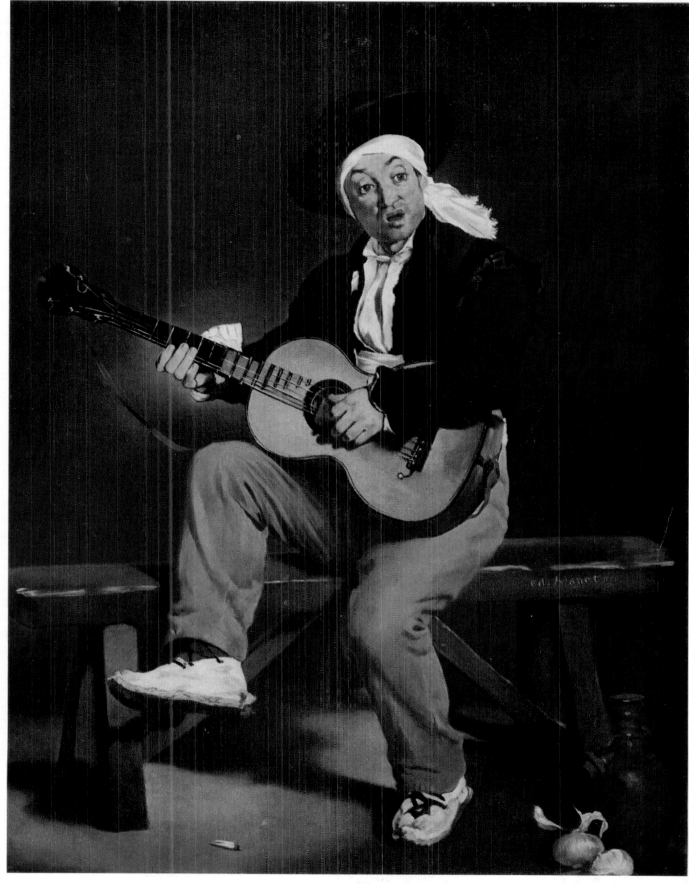

3. THE SPANISH SINGER. 1860. Also known as 'Le Guitarrero'. New York, Metropolitan Museum of Art
(Gift of William Church Osborn, 1949)

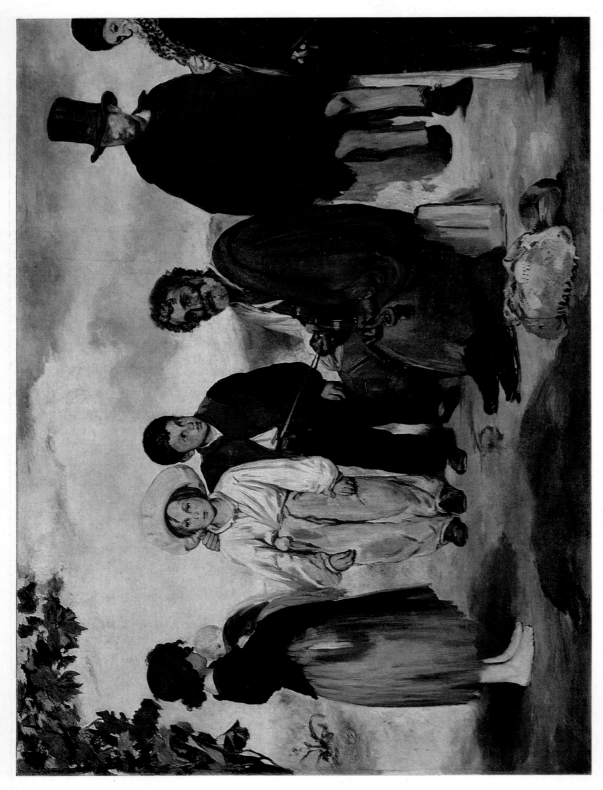

4. THE OLD MUSICIAN. 1861–2. Washington, National Gallery of Art (Chester Dale Collection)

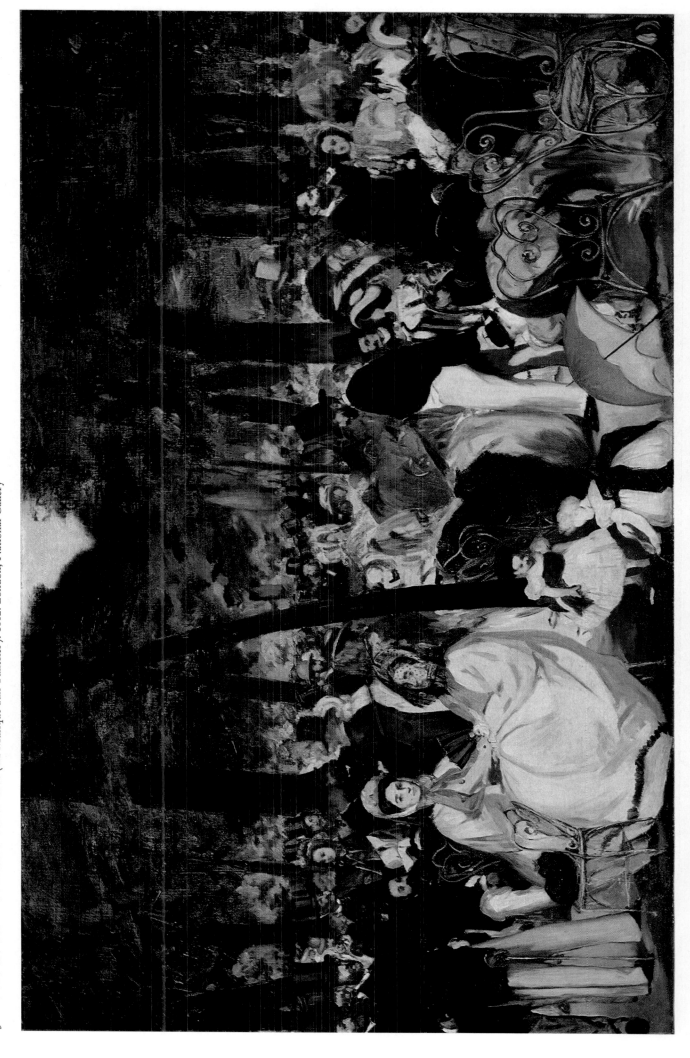

5. MUSIC IN THE TUILERIES GARDENS ('La Musique aux Tuileries'). 1862. London, National Gallery

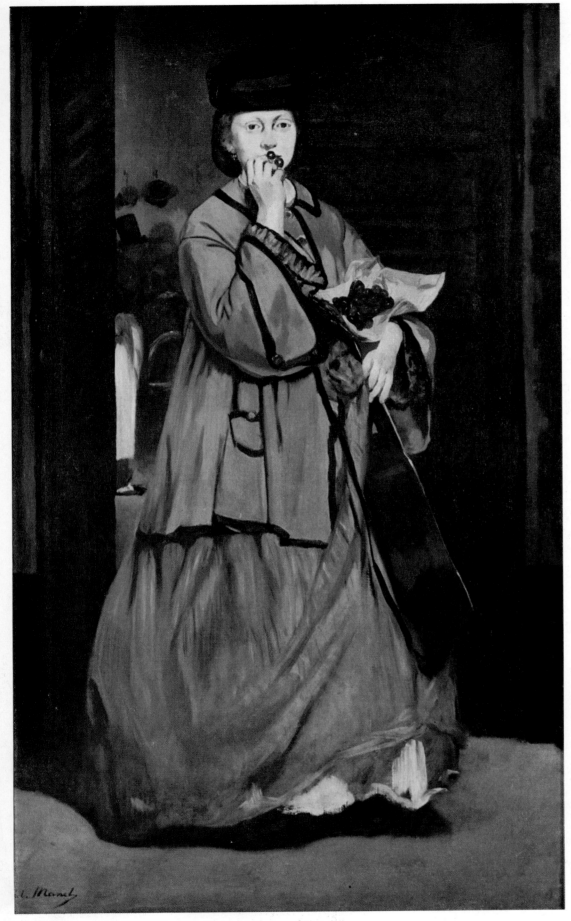

6. THE STREET SINGER. 1862. Boston, Museum of Fine Arts

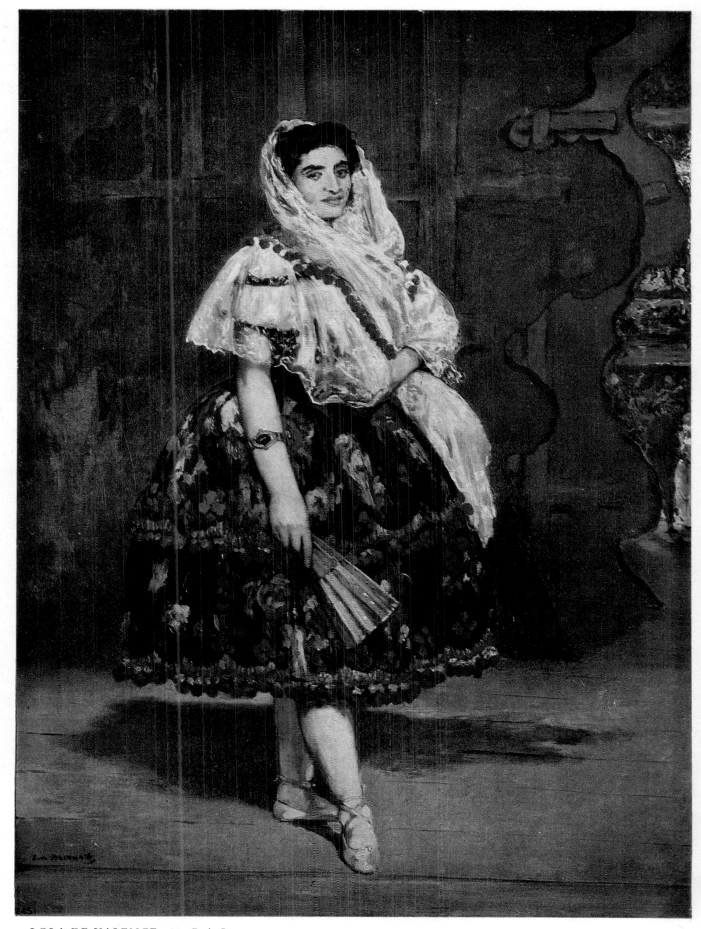

7. LOLA DE VALENCE. 1862. Paris, Louvre

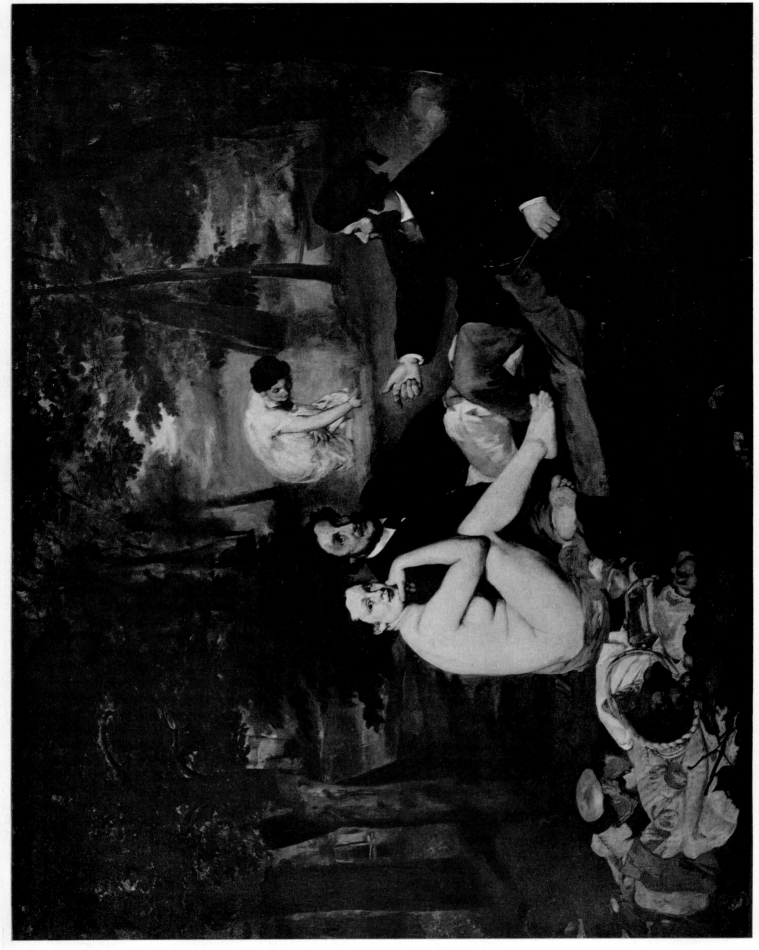

8. THE PICNIC ('Le Déjeuner sur l'Herbe'). 1862–3. Paris, Louvre

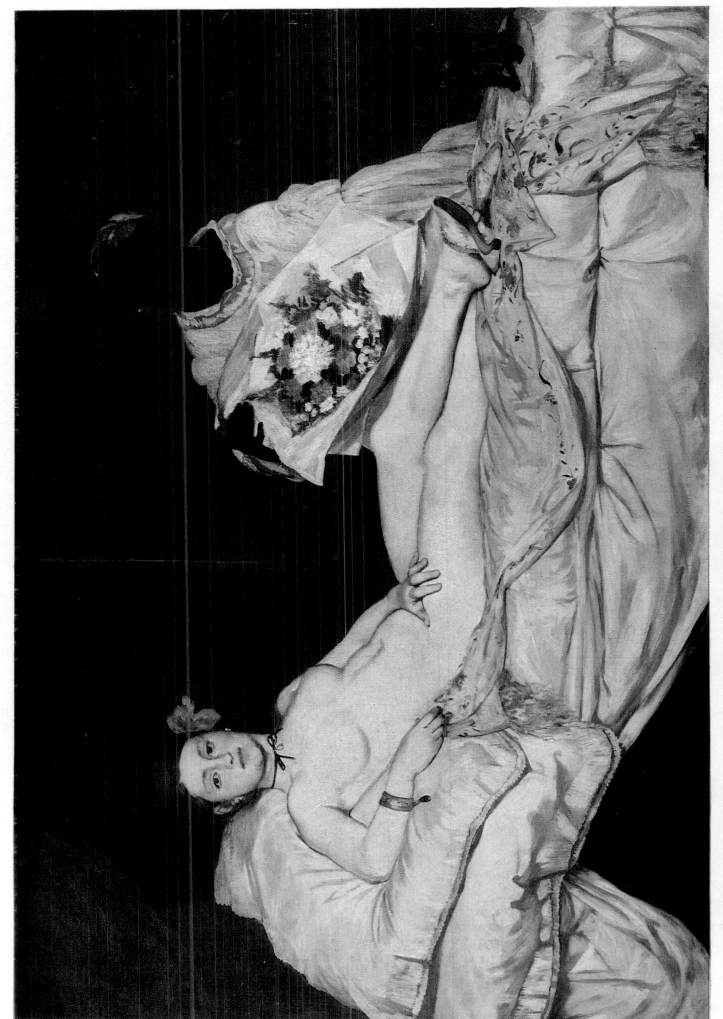

9. OLYMPIA. 1863. Paris, Louvre

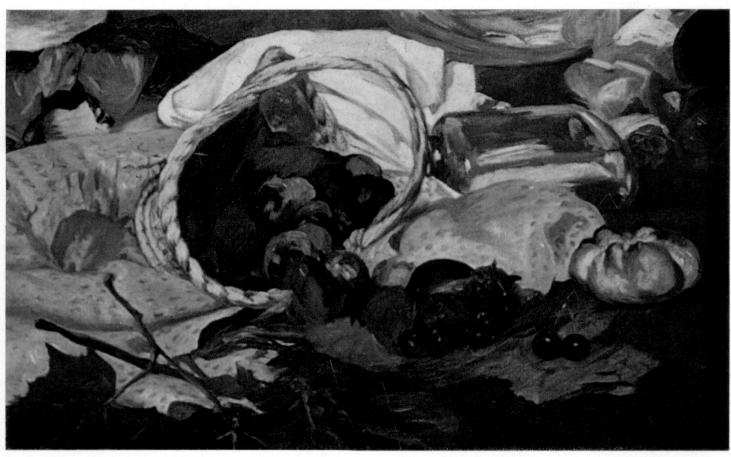

10. Detail of Plate 8

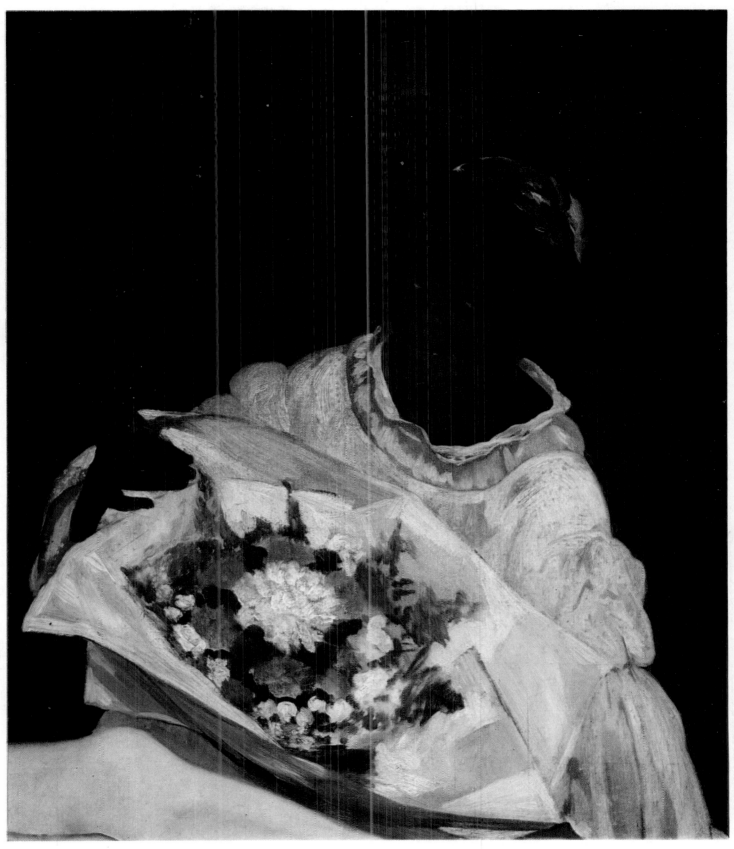

11. Detail of Plate 9

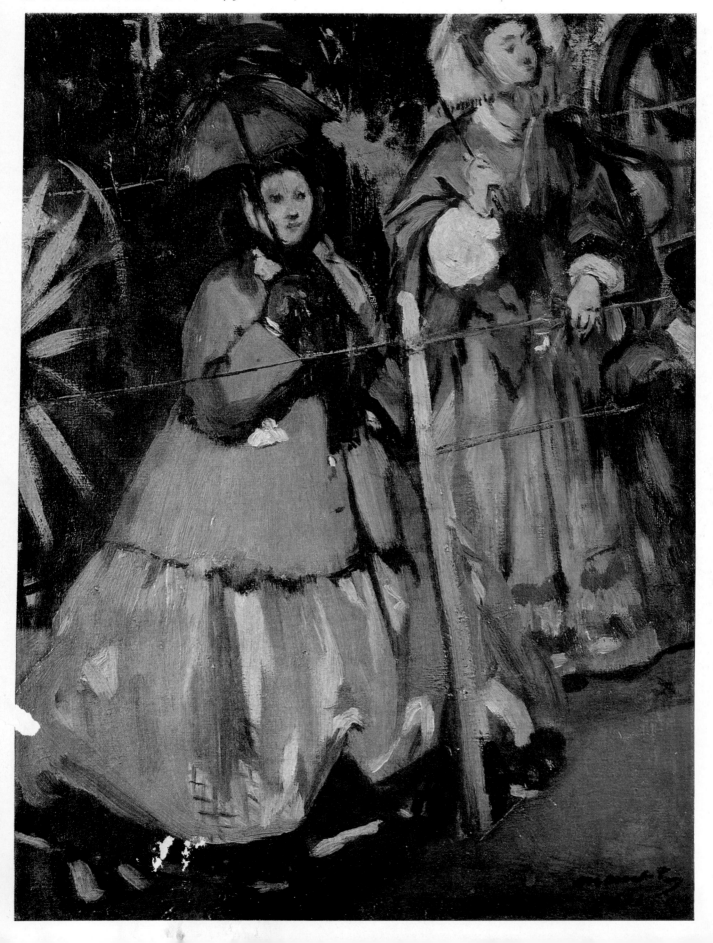

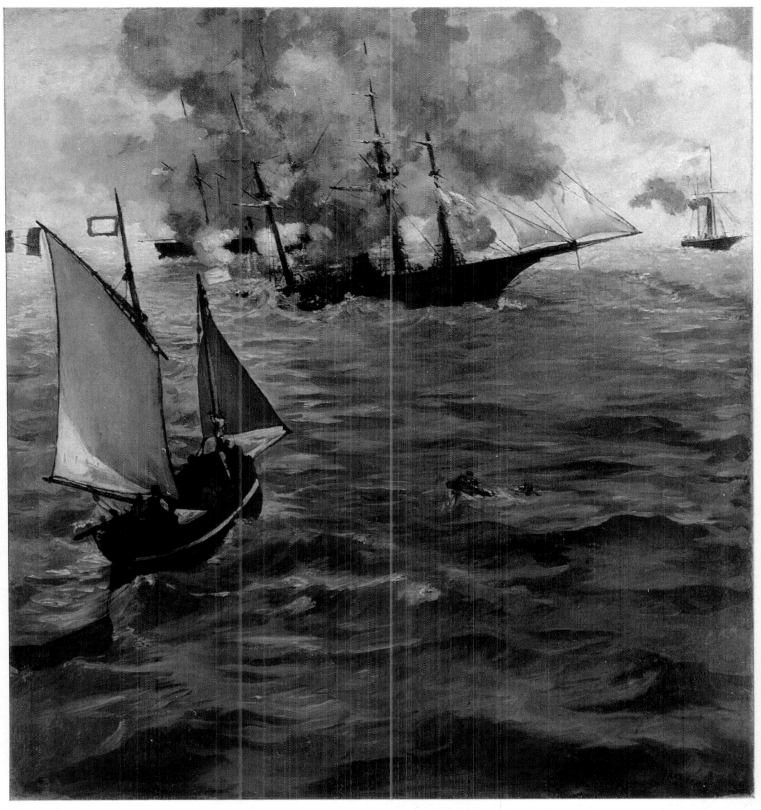

13. THE BATTLE OF THE KEARSARGE AND THE ALABAMA. 1864. Philadelphia, John G. Johnson Collection

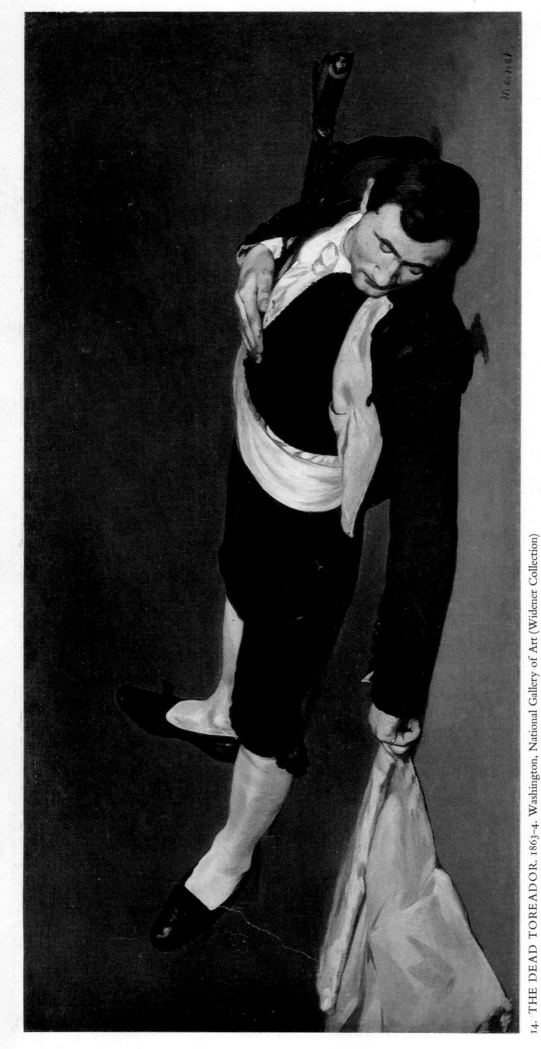

14. THE DEAD TOREADOR. 1863-4. Washington, National Gallery of Art (Widener Collection)

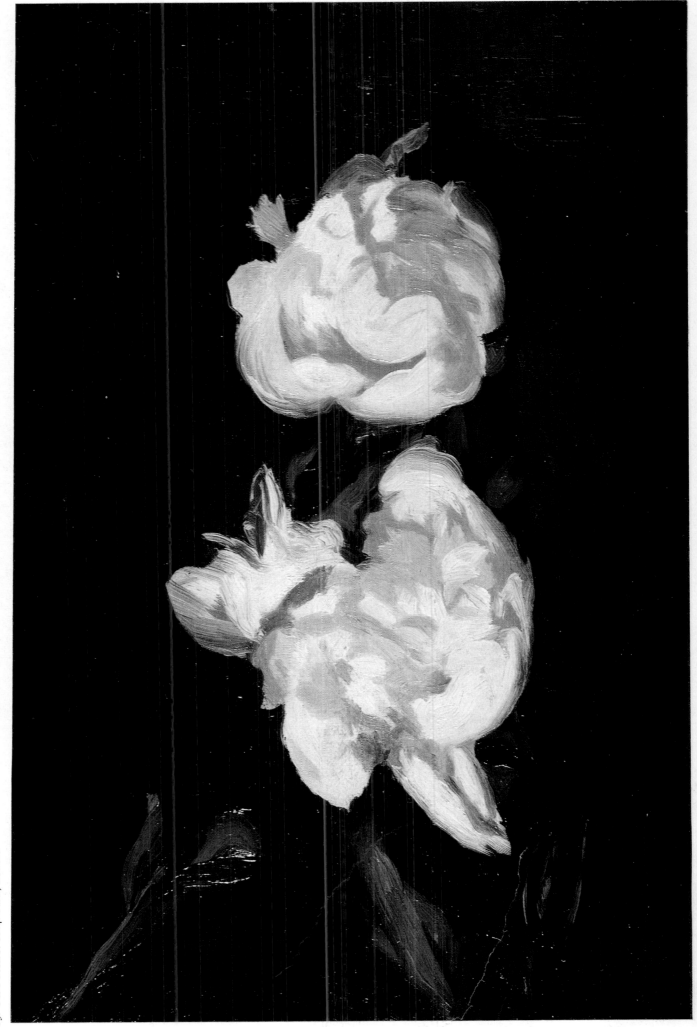

15. PEONIES. 1864. Paris, Louvre

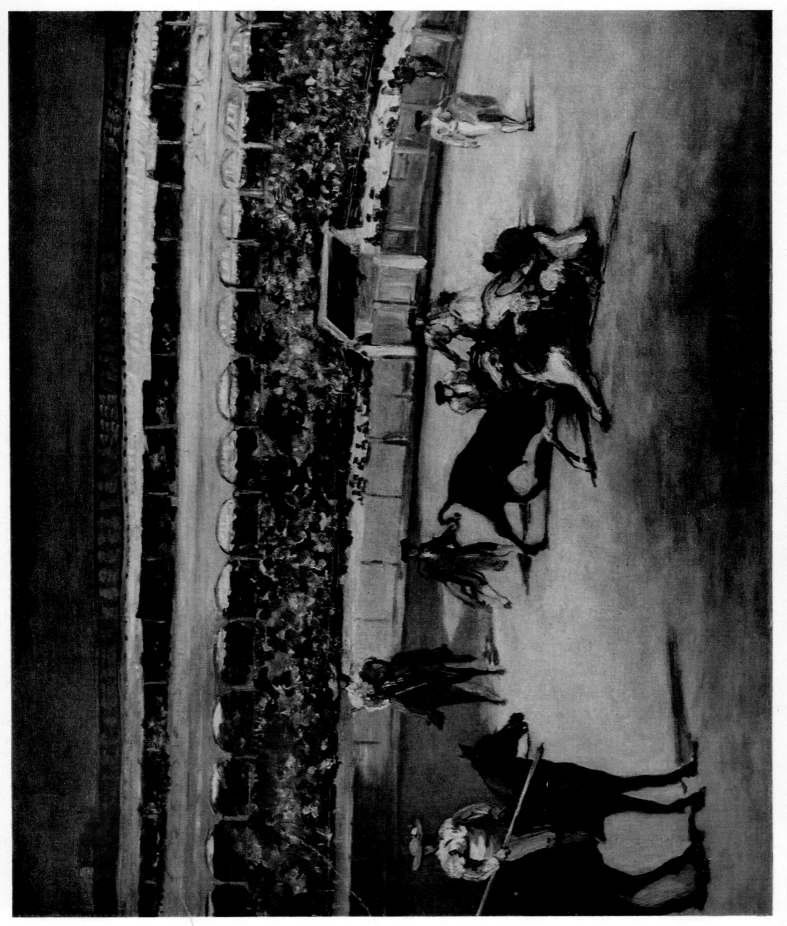

16. BULL-FIGHTING SCENE. 1865–6. Paris, Heirs of Baroness Goldschmidt-Rothschild

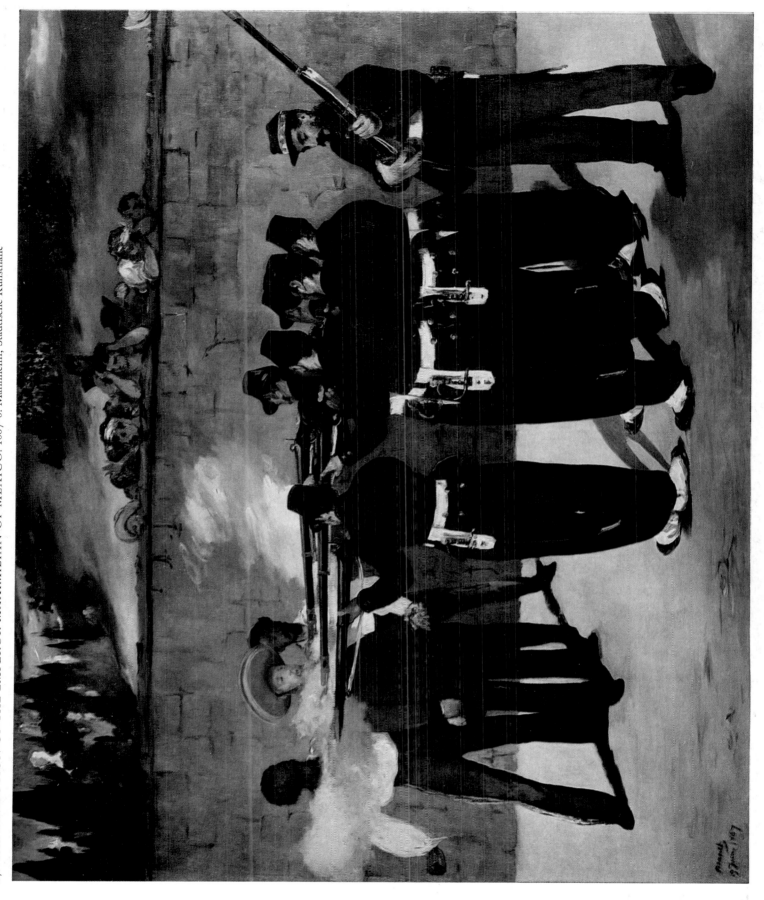

17. THE EXECUTION OF THE EMPEROR MAXIMILIAN OF MEXICO. 1867–8. Mannheim, Städtische Kunsthalle

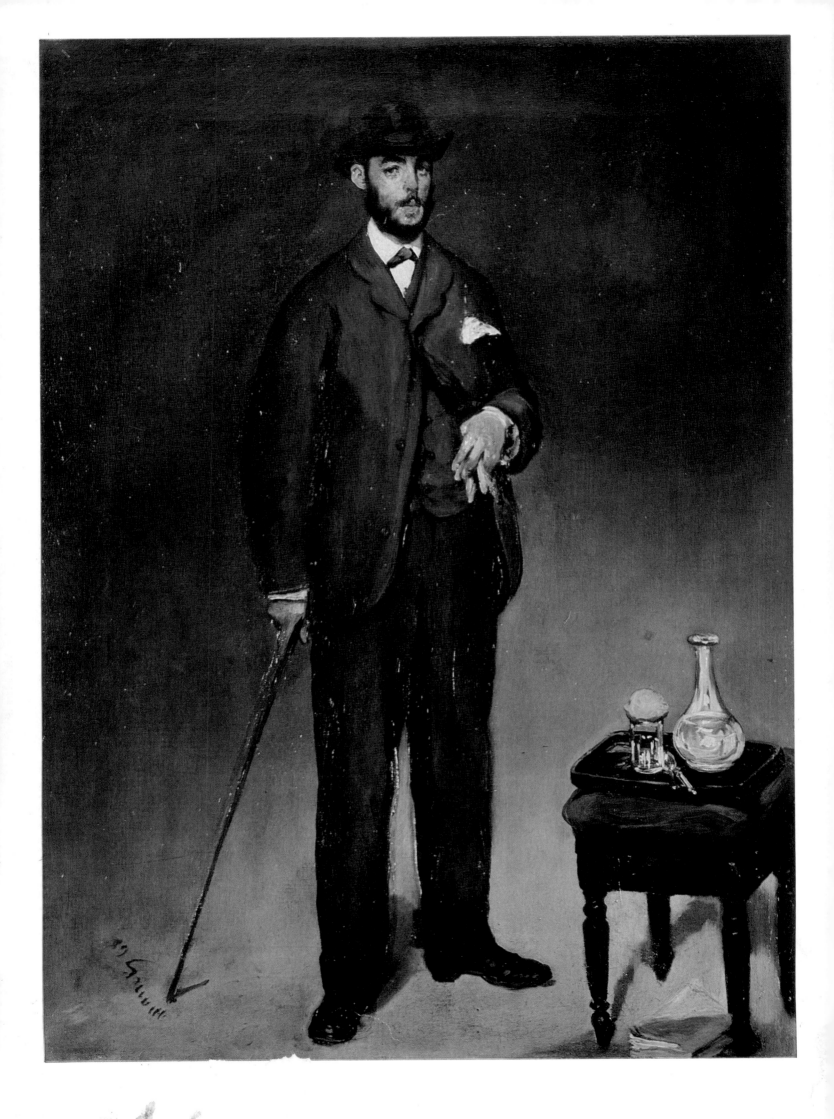

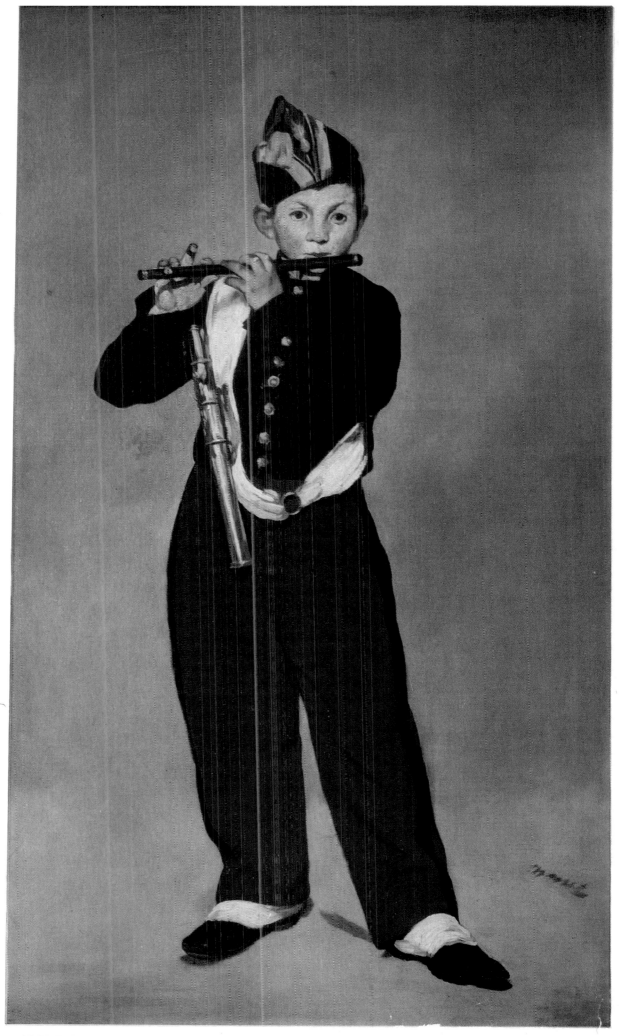

19. THE FIFER. 1866. Paris, Louvre

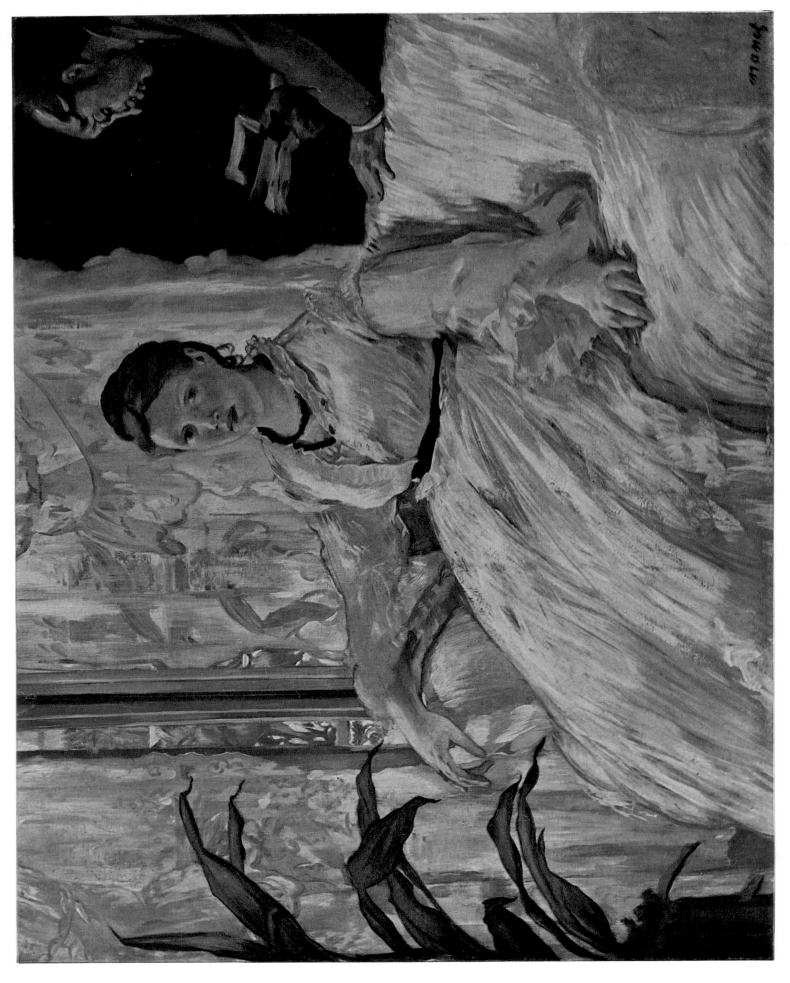

20. THE READING. 1869. Paris, Louvre

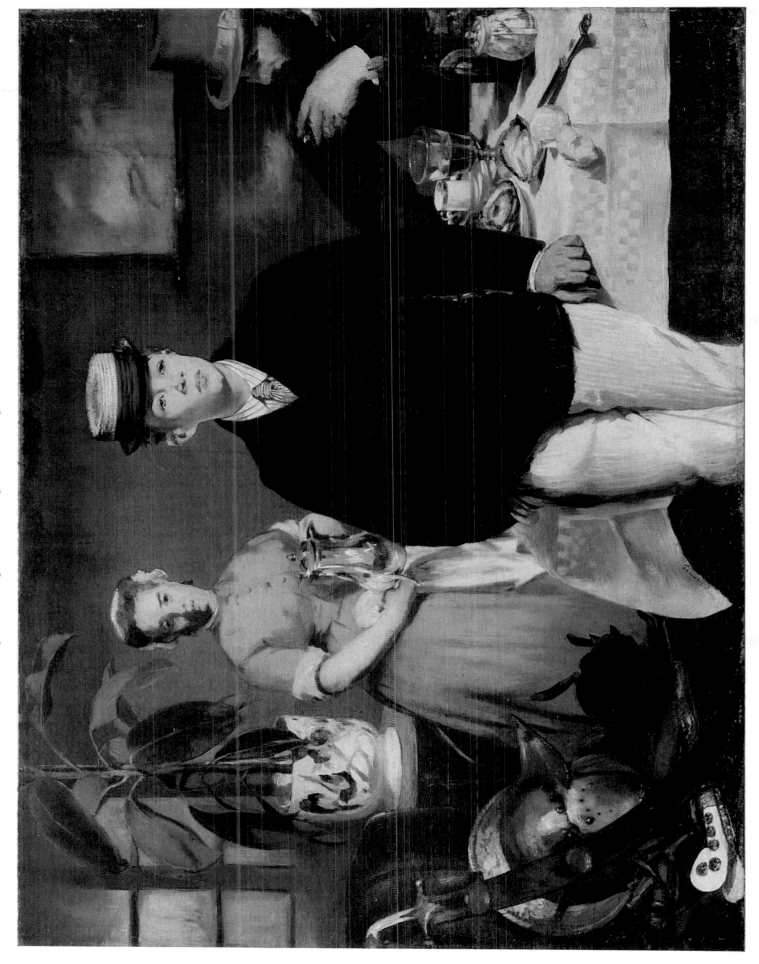

21. LUNCHEON IN THE STUDIO. 1868. Munich, Bayerische Staatsgemäldesammlungen (Neue Staatsgalerie)

22. STILL LIFE WITH SALMON. 1866–9. Shelburne Museum, Shelburne, Vermont (The Electra Havemeyer Webb Fund)

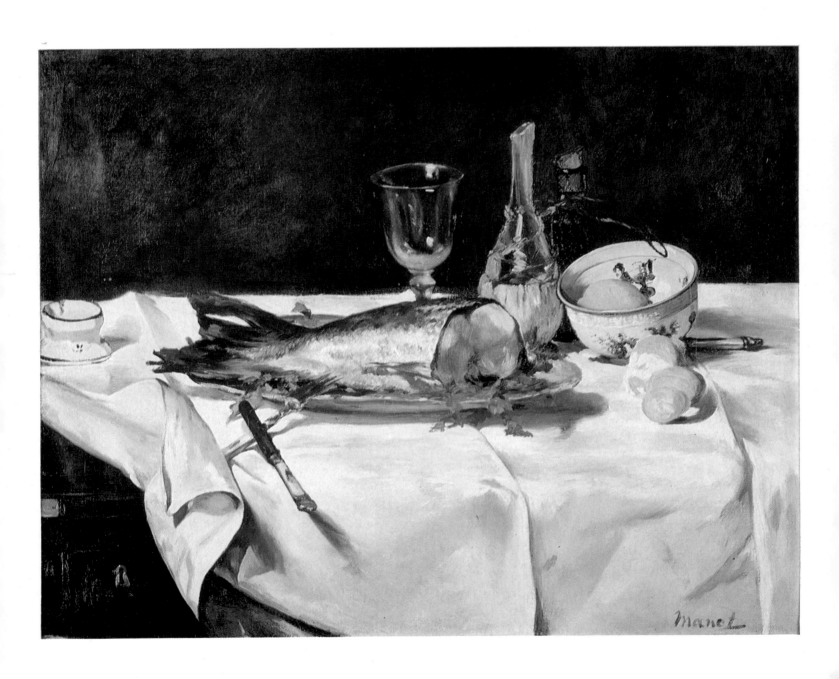

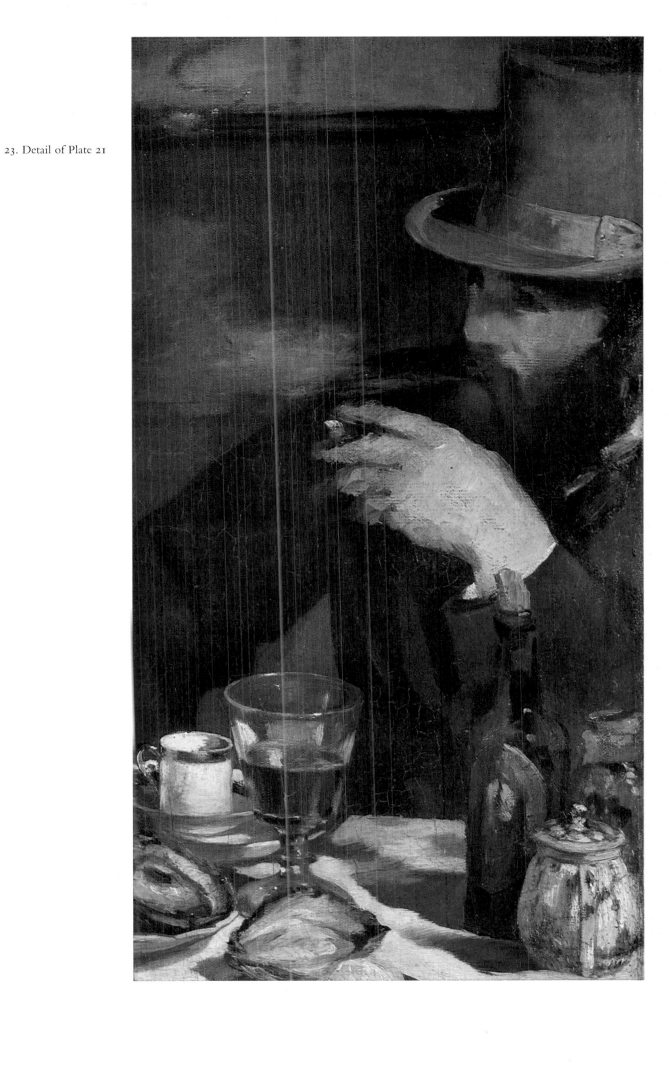

23. Detail of Plate 21

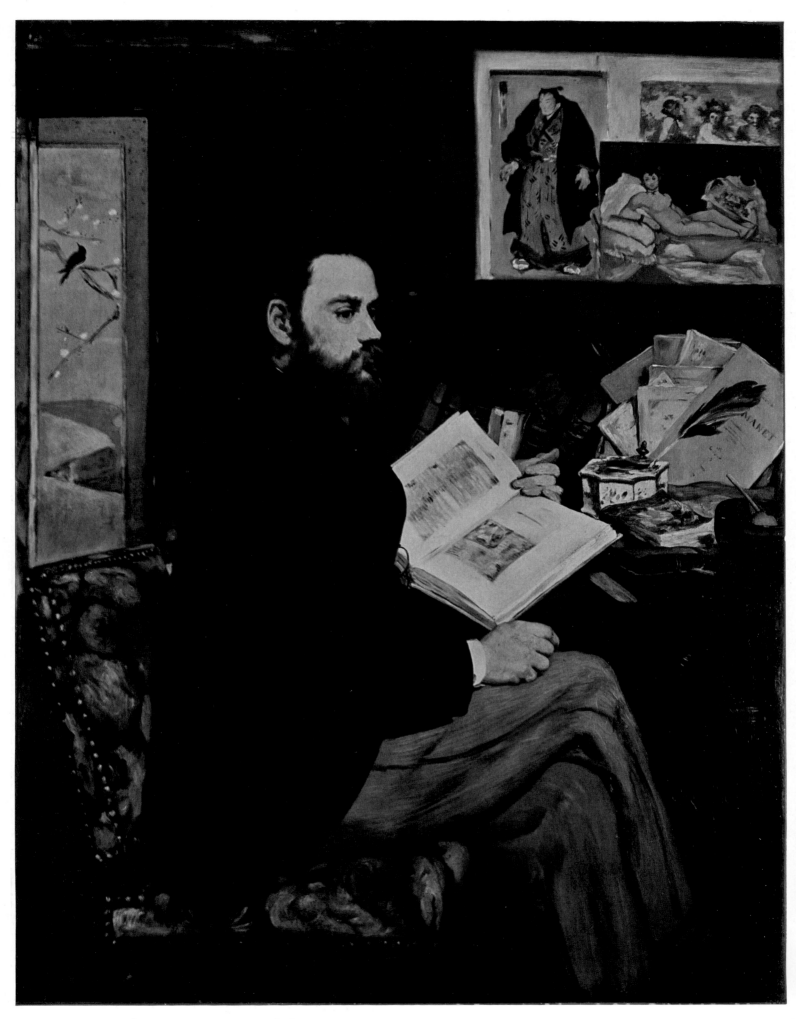

24. PORTRAIT OF ÉMILE ZOLA. 1867–8. Paris, Louvre

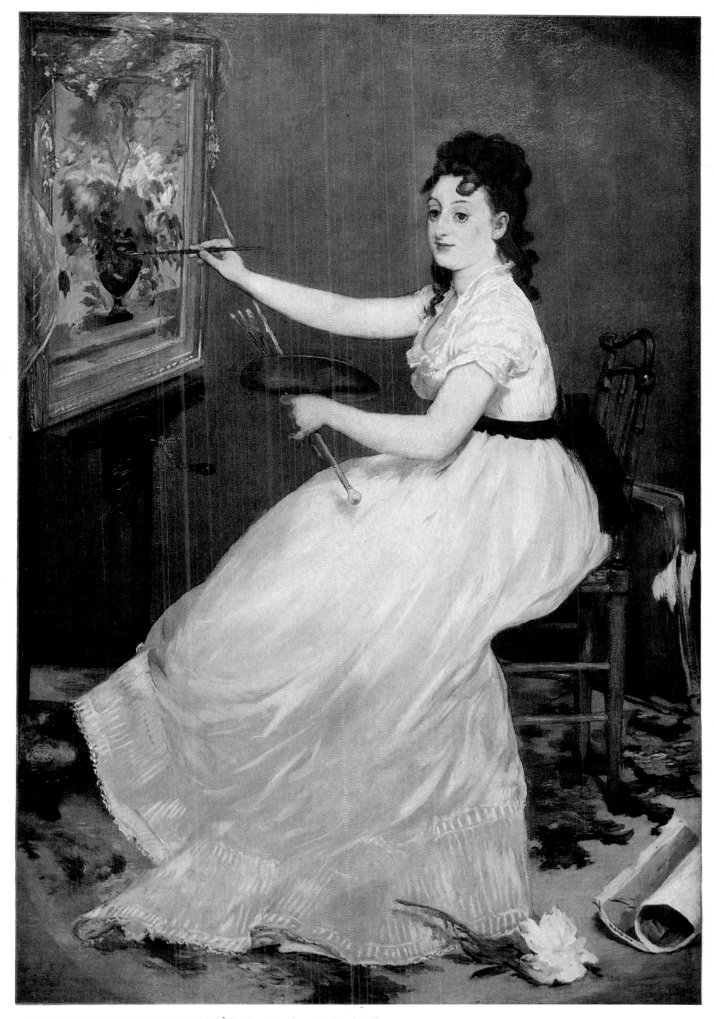

25. PORTRAIT OF EVA GONZALÈS. 1870. London, National Gallery

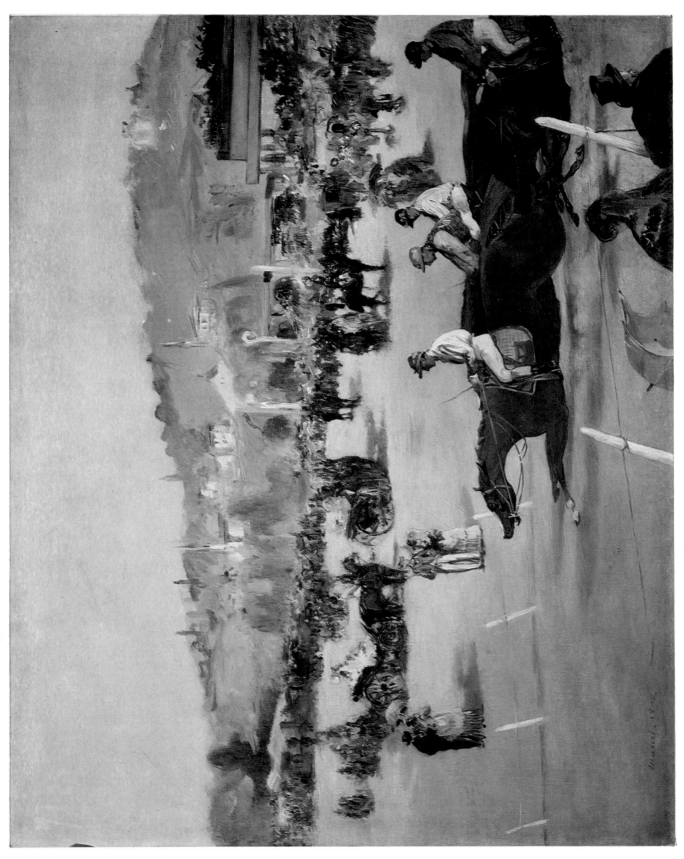

26. RACECOURSE IN THE BOIS DE BOULOGNE. 1872. New York, Mr. John Hay Whitney

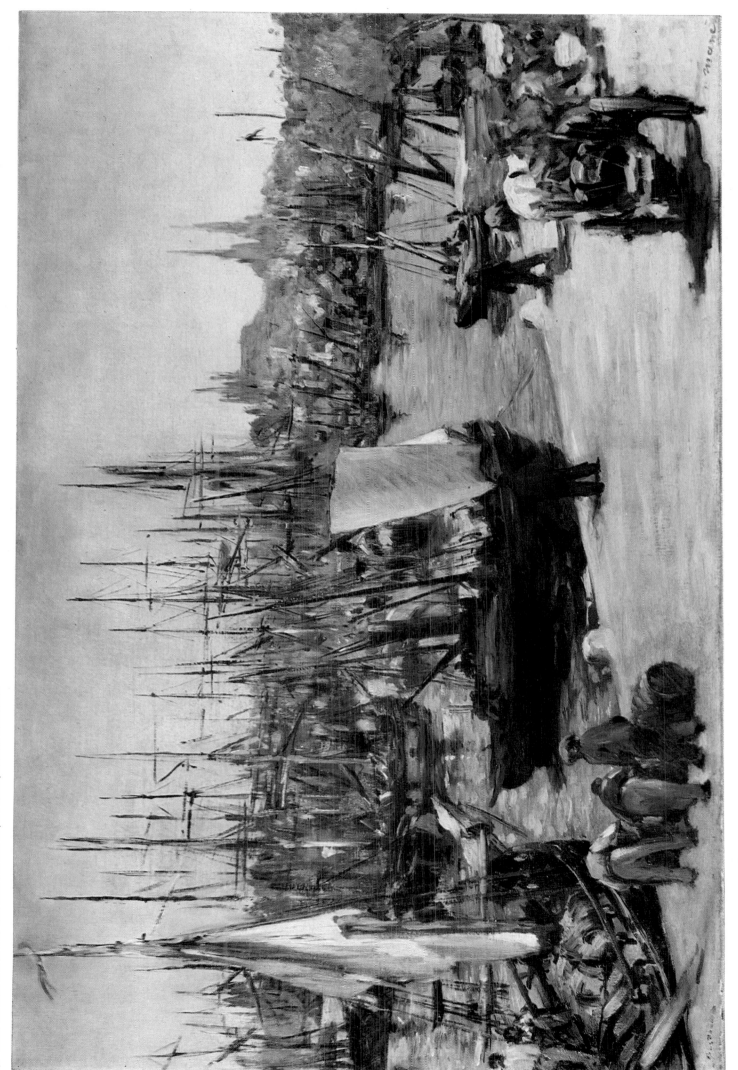

27. THE HARBOUR AT BORDEAUX. 1871. Zürich, Bührle Collection

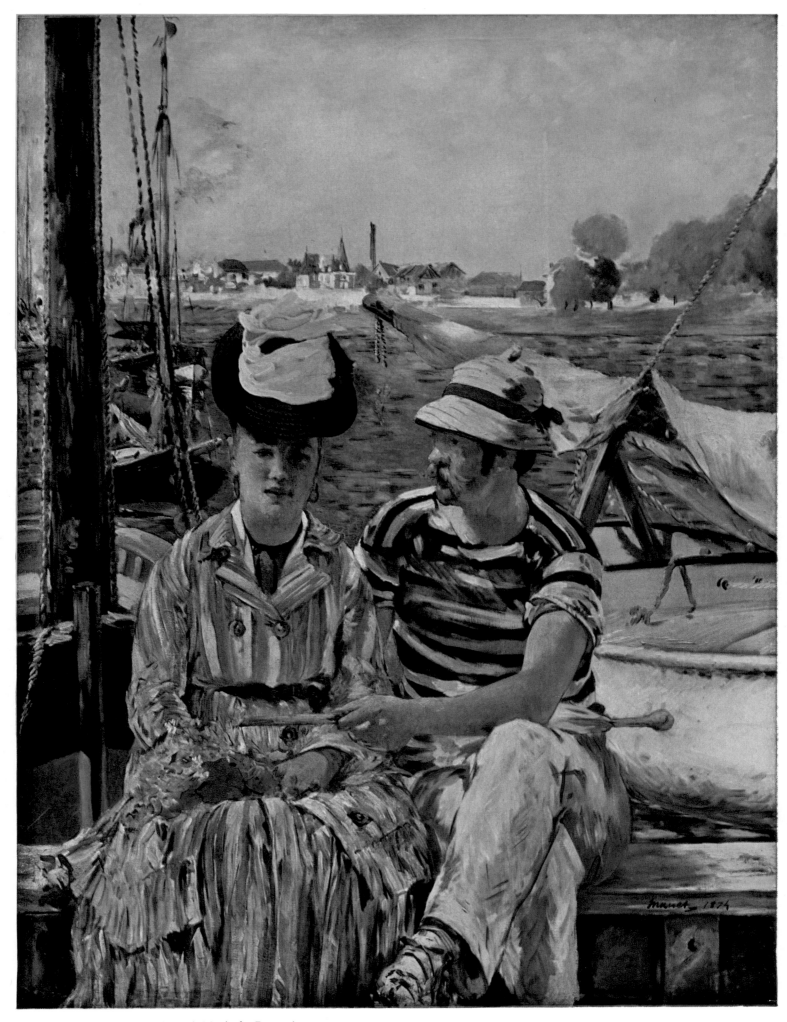

28. ARGENTEUIL. 1874. Tournai, Musée des Beaux-Arts

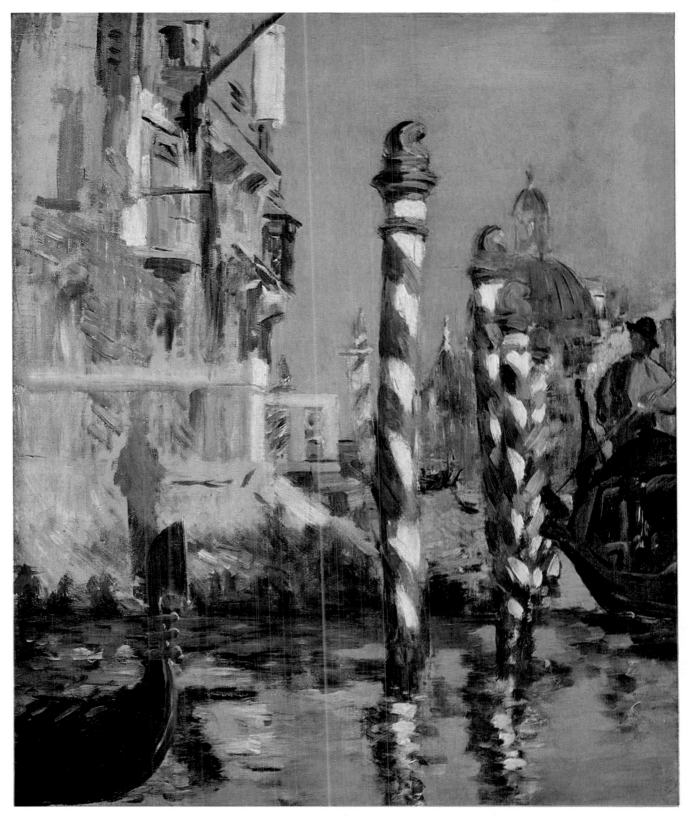

29. THE GRAND CANAL, VENICE. 1874. San Francisco, The Provident Securities Company

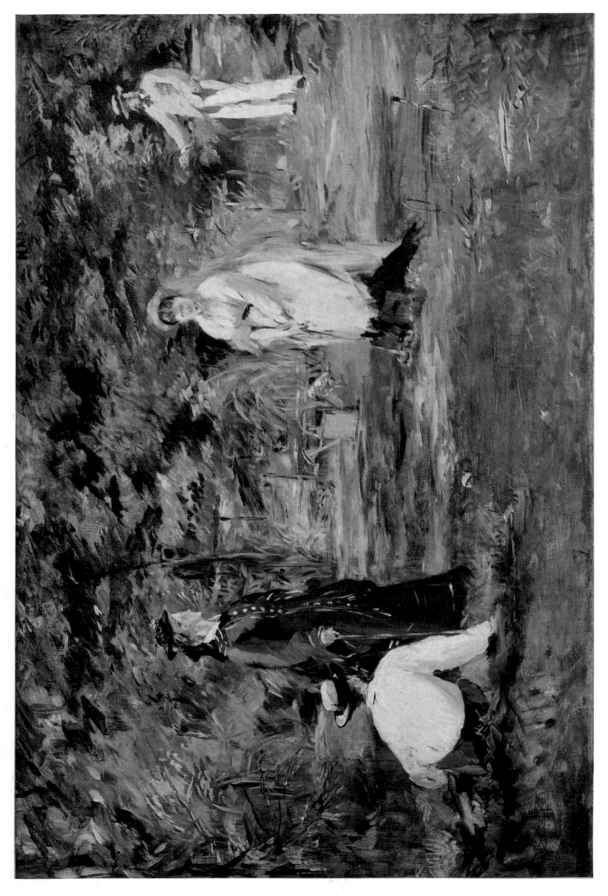

30. THE GAME OF CROQUET. 1873. Frankfurt, Städelsches Kunstinstitut

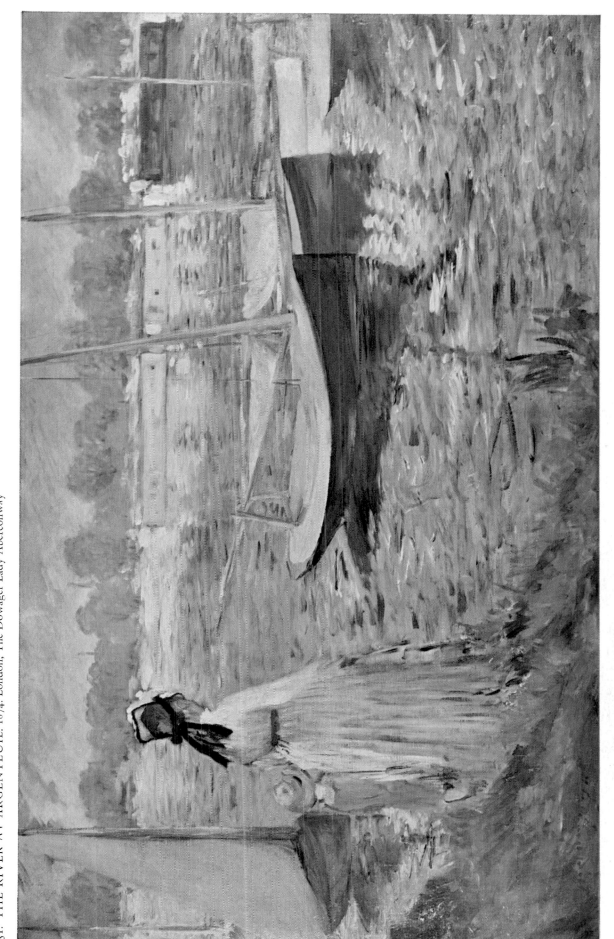

31. THE RIVER AT ARGENTEUIL. 1874. London, The Dowager Lady Aberconway

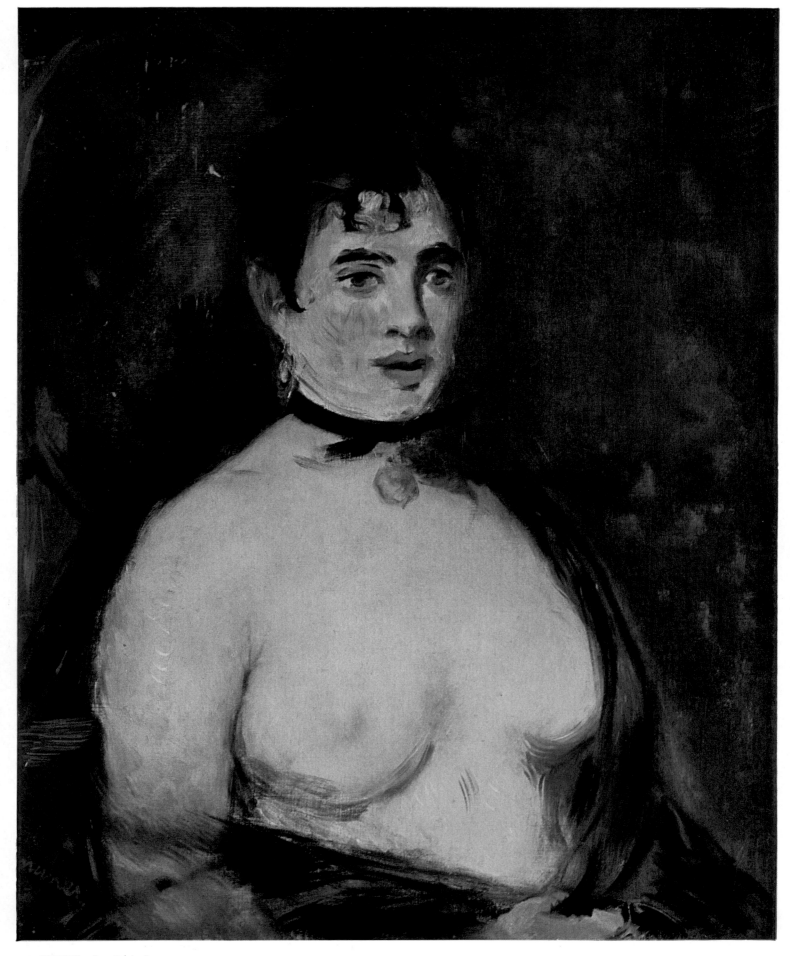

32. NUDE. 1875. Paris, Louvre

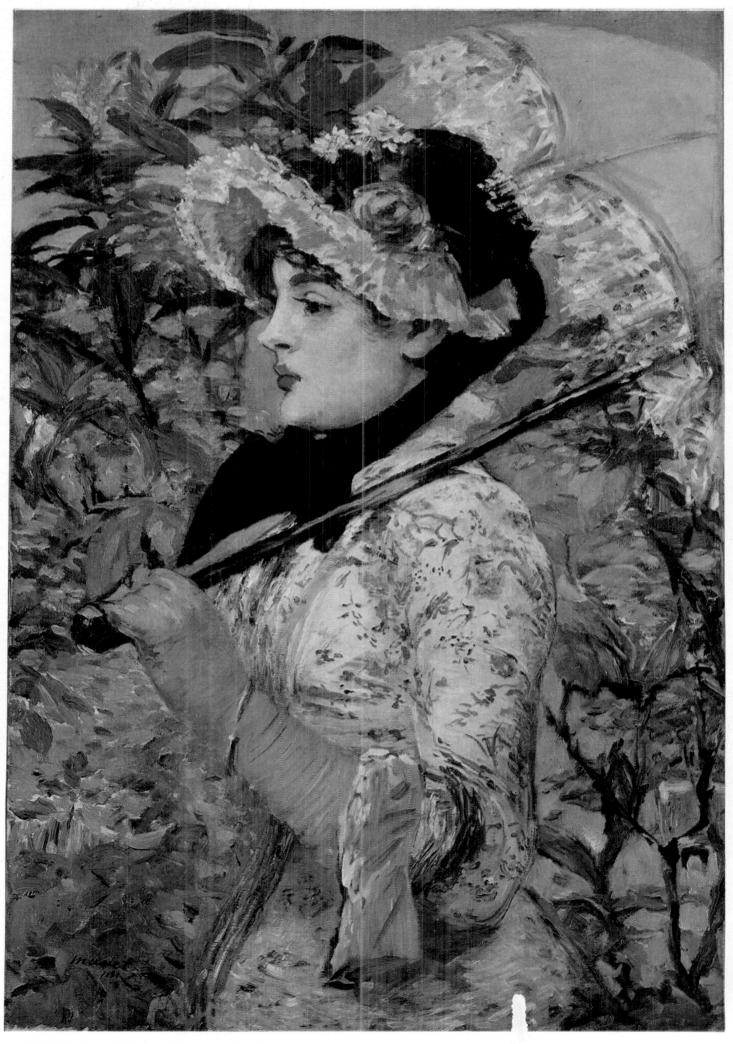

33. SPRING: JEANNE. 1881. New York, Mrs. Harry Payne Bingham

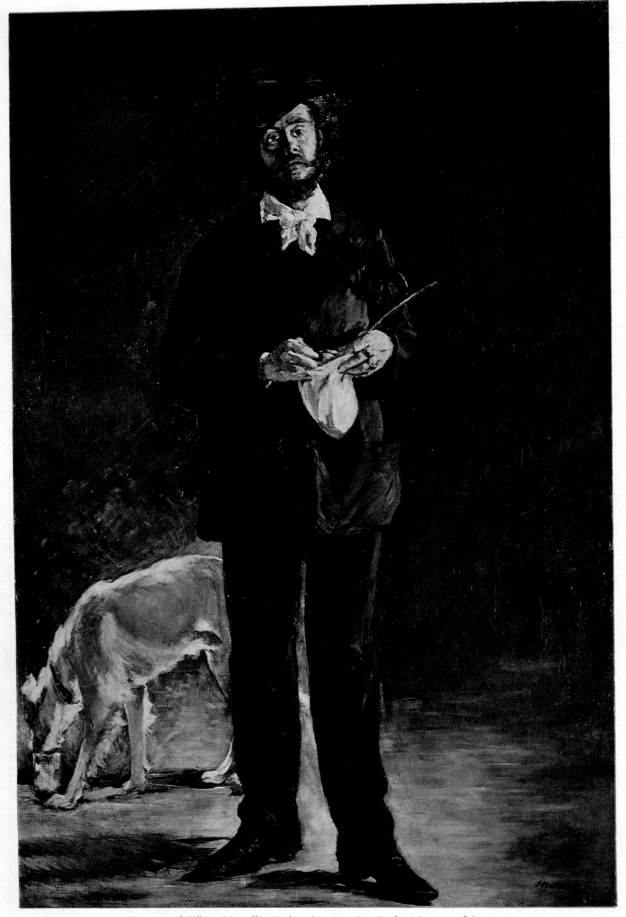

34. THE ARTIST – Portrait of Gilbert-Marcellin Desboutin. 1875. São Paulo, Museum of **Art**

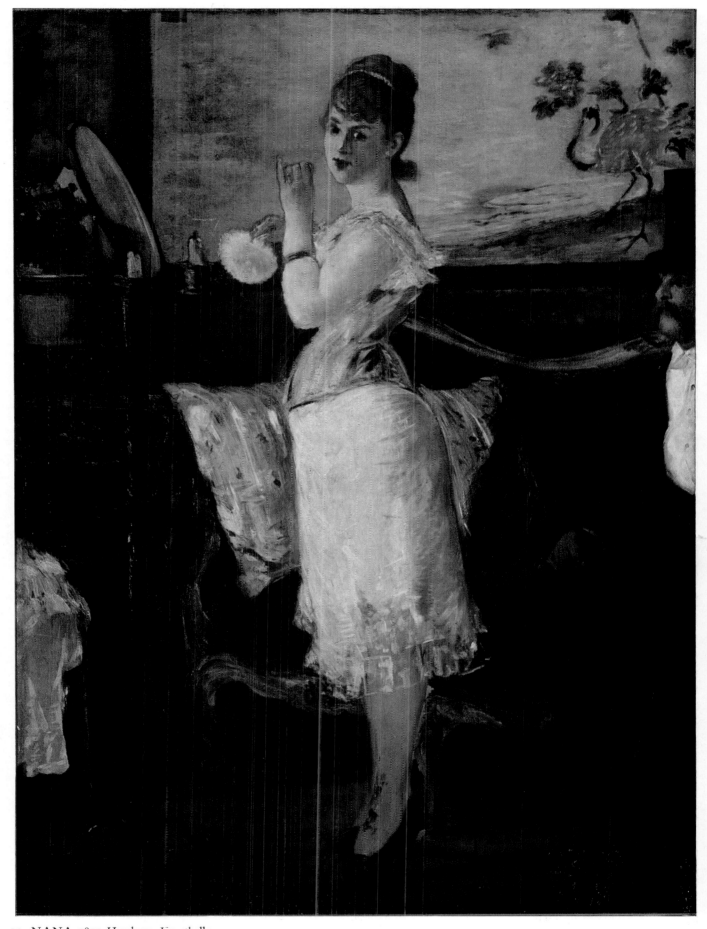

35. NANA. 1877. Hamburg, Kunsthalle

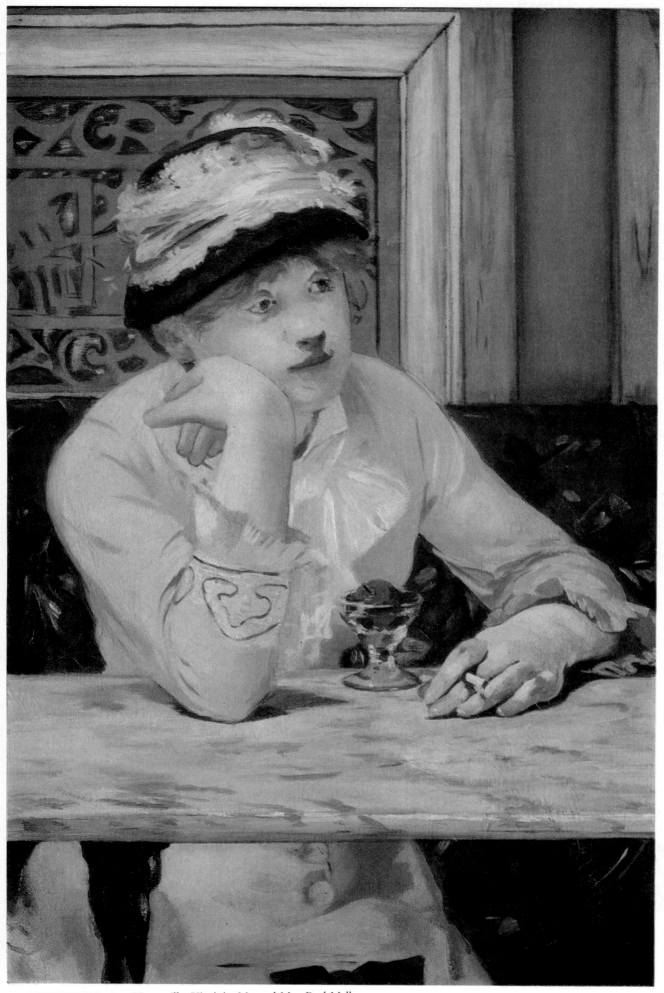

36. THE PLUM. 1877. Upperville, Virginia, Mr. and Mrs. Paul Mellon

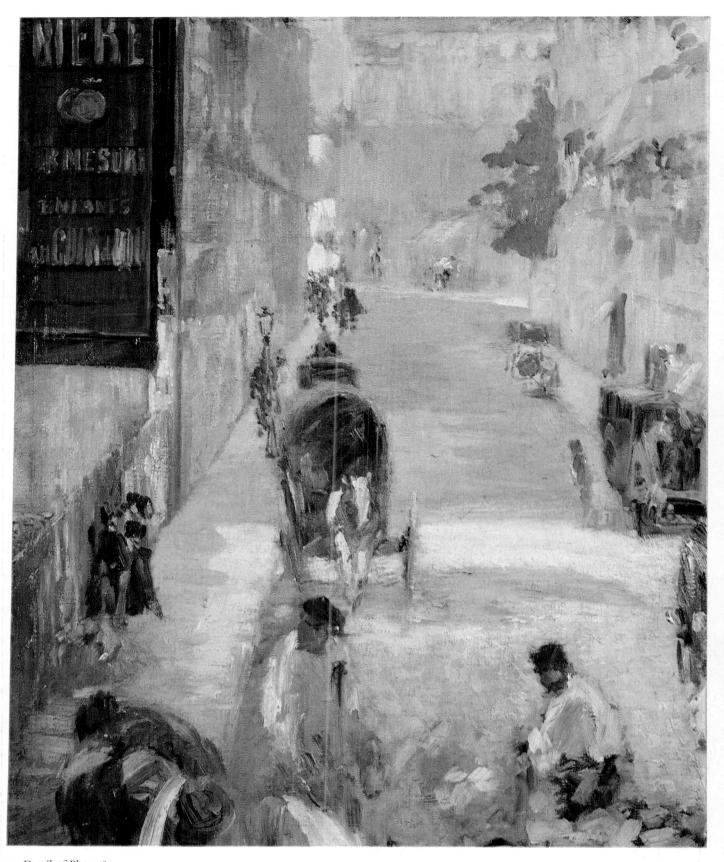

37. Detail of Plate 38

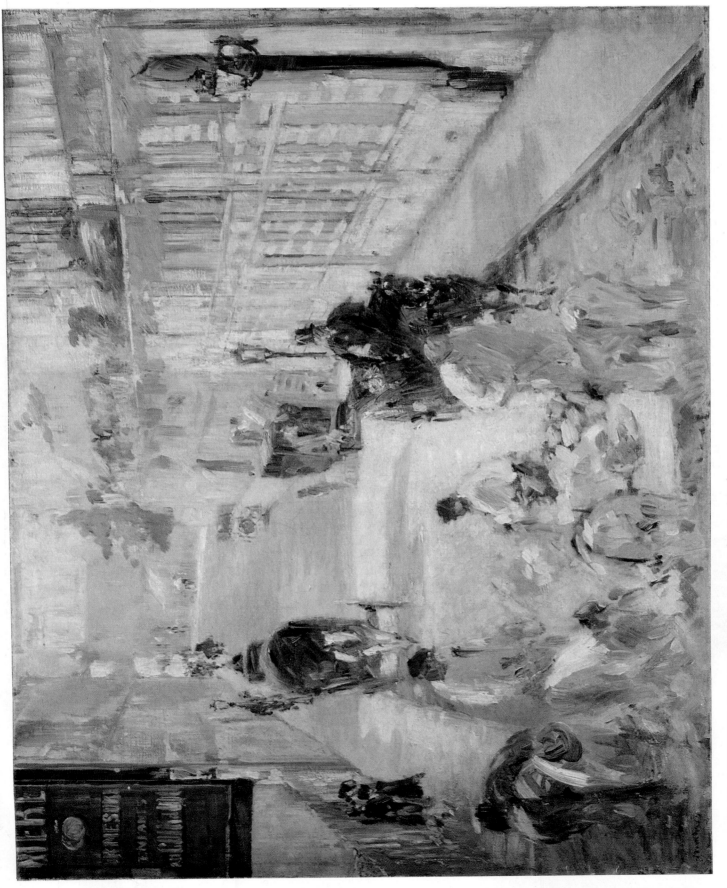

38. THE ROAD-MENDERS, RUE DE BERNE. 1878. London, Lord Butler

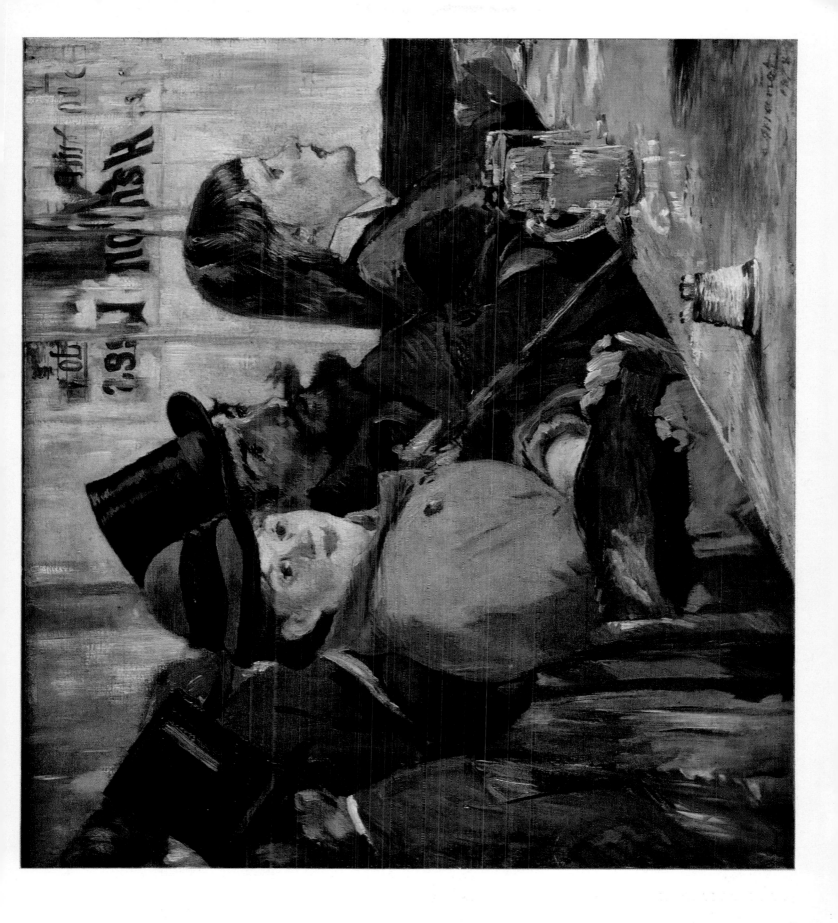

39. AT THE CAFÉ. 1878.

Winterthur, Stiftung Dr. Oskar Reinhart

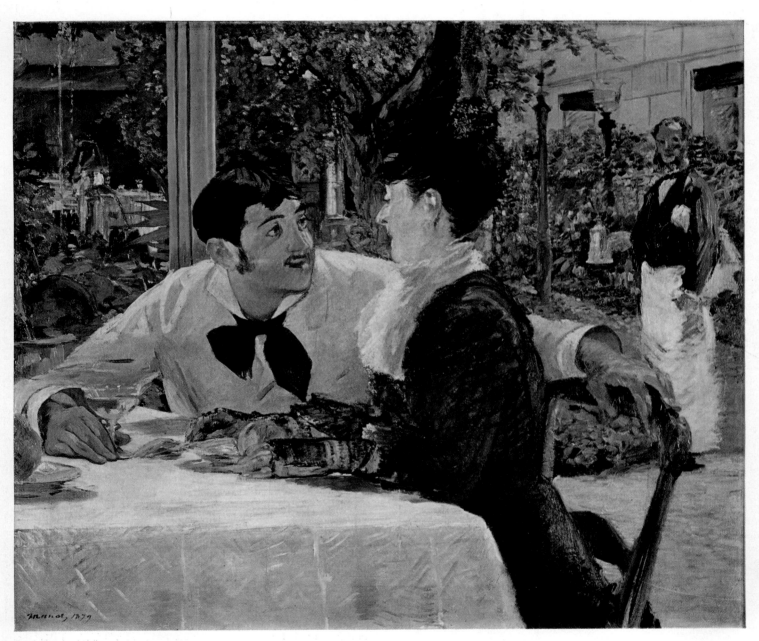

40. AT PÈRE LATHUILLE'S. 1879. Tournai, Musée des Beaux-Arts

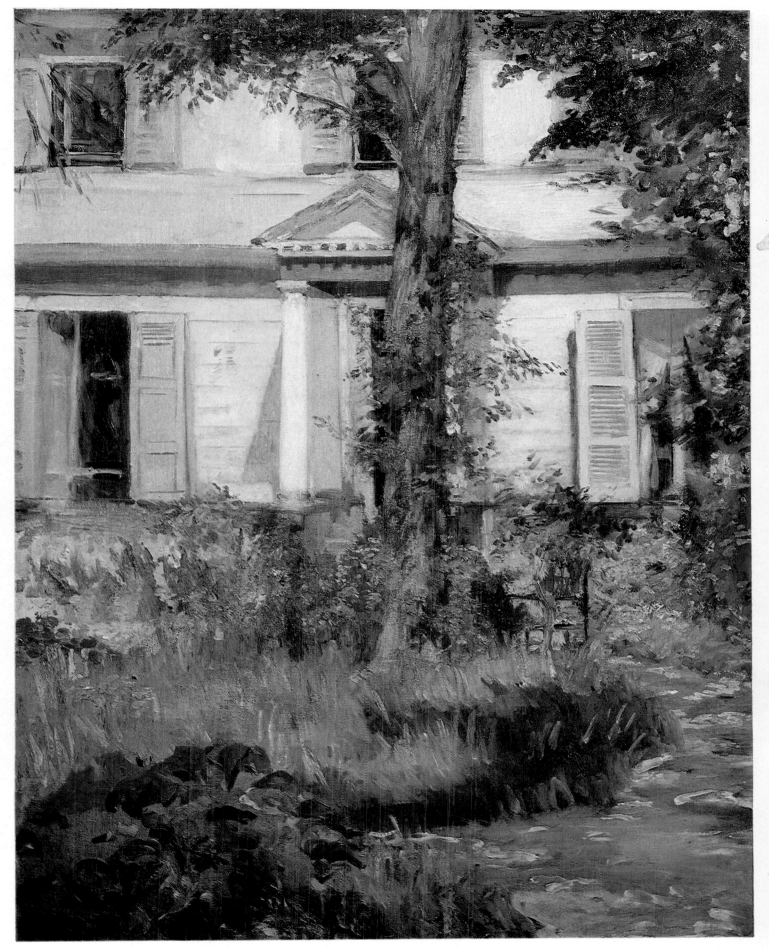

41. VILLA AT RUEIL. 1882. Melbourne, National Gallery of Victoria

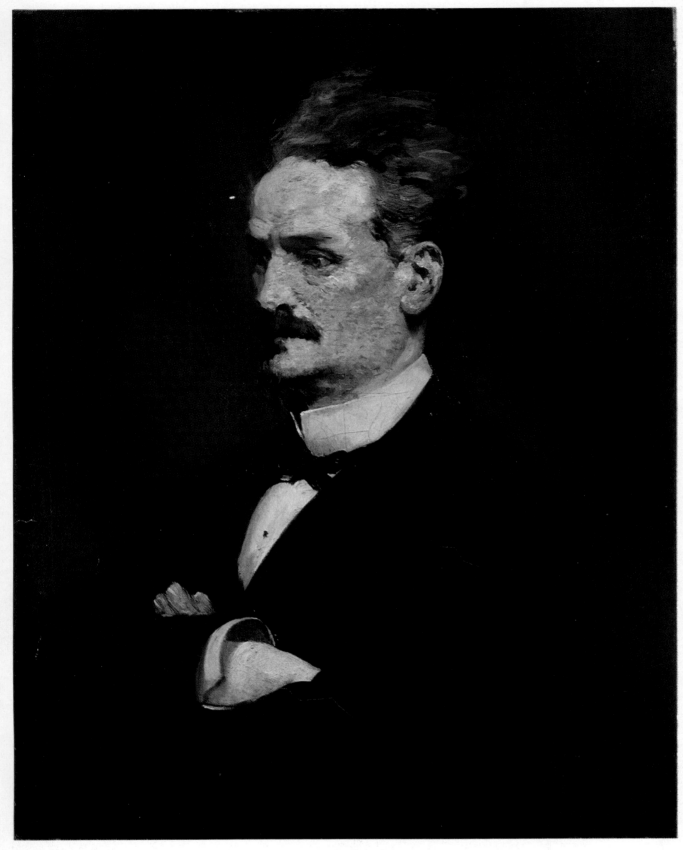

42. PORTRAIT OF HENRI ROCHEFORT. 1881. Hamburg, Kunsthalle

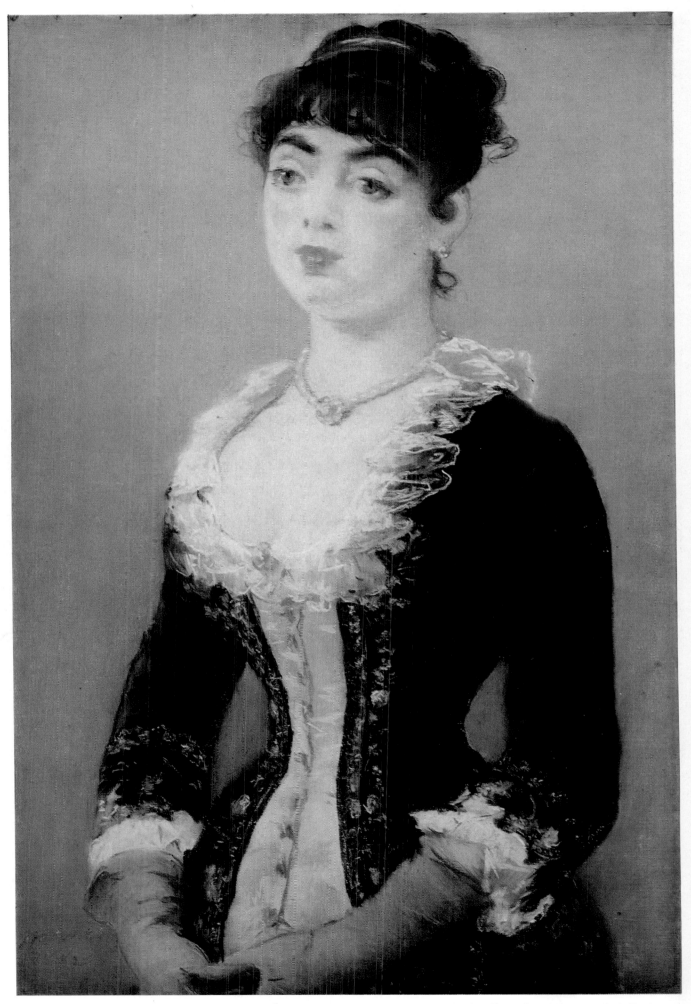

43. PORTRAIT OF MADAME MICHEL-LÉVY. Pastel, 1882. Washington, National Gallery of Art (Chester Dale Collection)

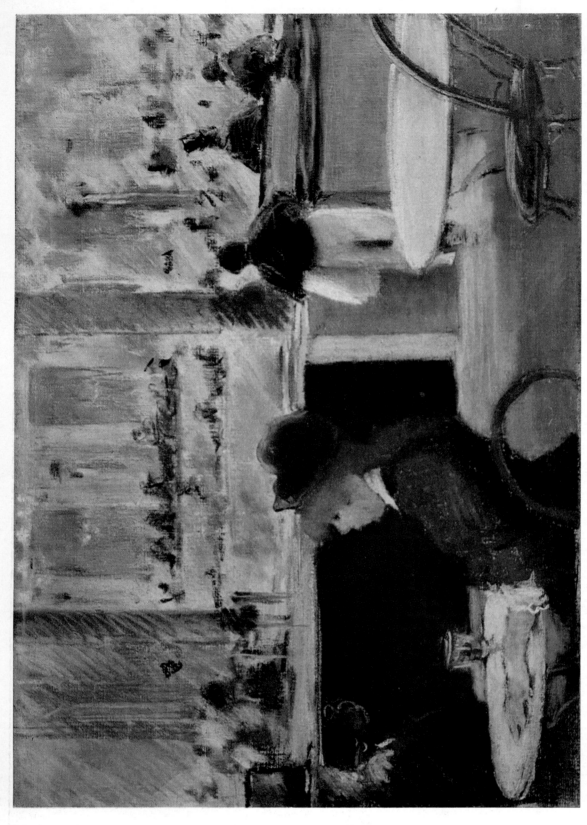

44. INTERIOR OF A CAFÉ. Oil and Pastel. c. 1880. Glasgow, City Art Gallery (Burrell Collection)

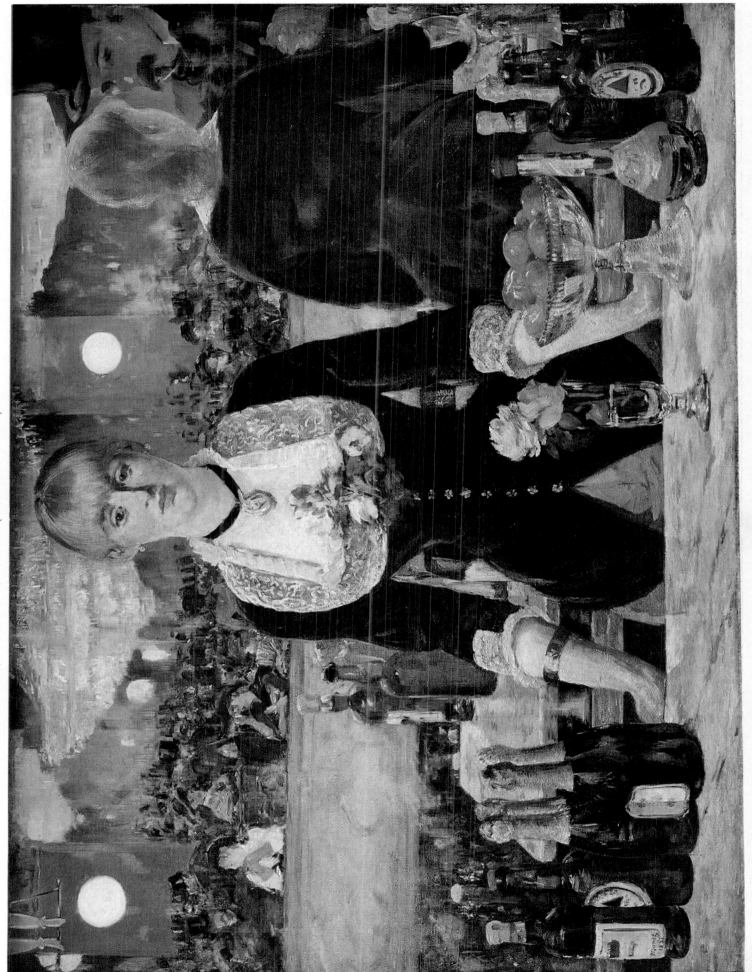

45. A BAR AT THE FOLIES-BERGÈRE. 1881–2. London, Courtauld Institute Galleries (Home House Trustees)

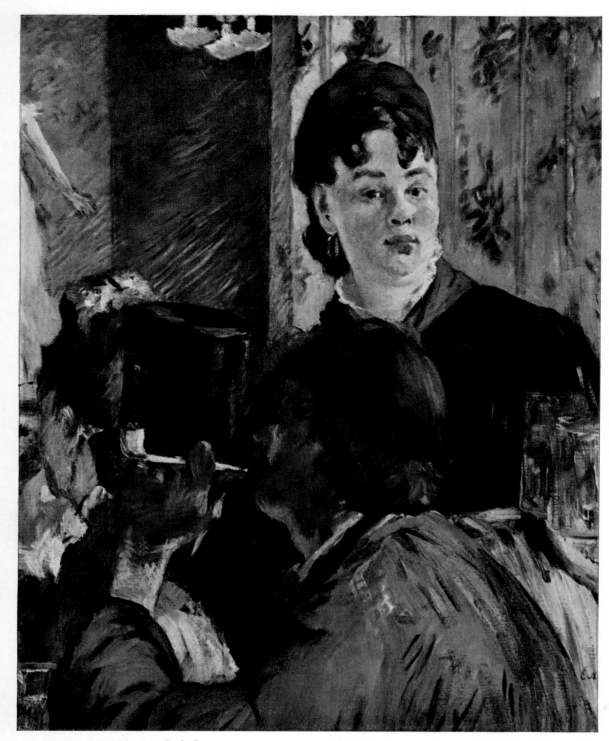

46. THE WAITRESS. 1878. Paris, Louvre

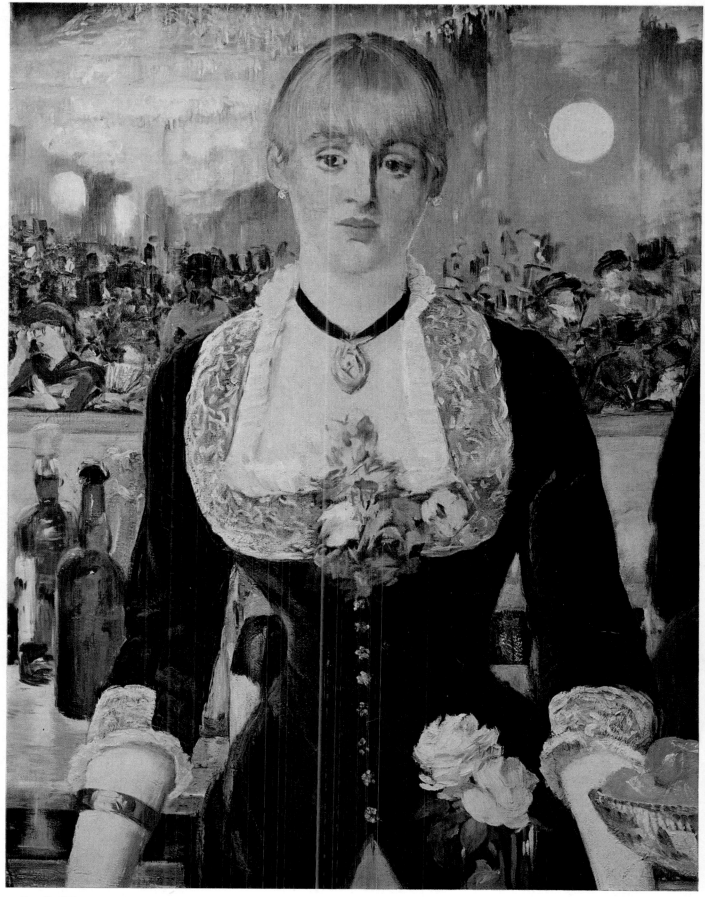

47. Detail of Plate 45

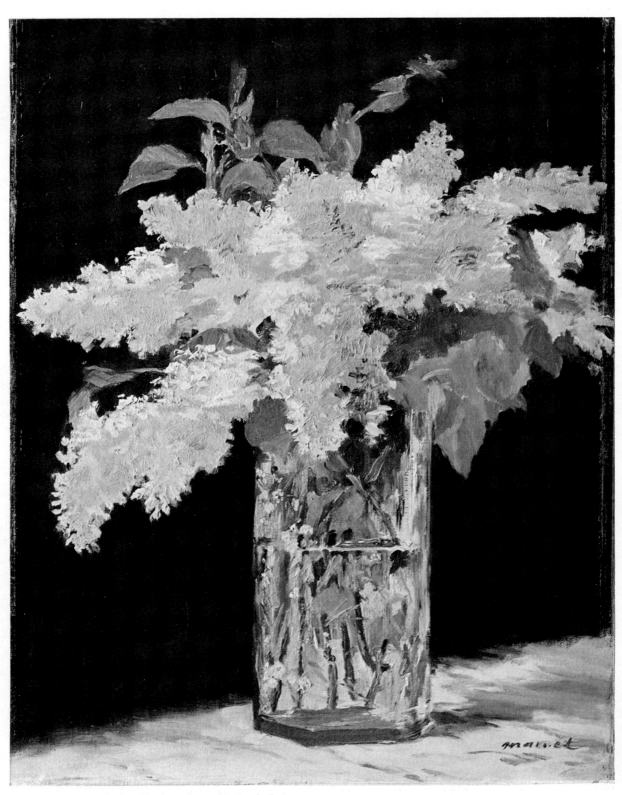

48. LILAC. 1883. Berlin–Charlottenburg, Nationalgalerie

NOTES ON THE PLATES

CHRONOLOGY

1832   January 23. Birth of Édouard Manet in Paris. His mother was the daughter of a French diplomat, his father, Auguste Manet, Chief of Personnel at the Ministry of Justice.

1842   Enters the Collège Rollin and meets Antonin Proust, who was to be a lifelong friend.

1848–9   Abortive naval career.

1850   Enters the studio of Thomas Couture.

1856   Leaves Couture's studio. Travels in Belgium, Holland, Germany, Austria and Italy.

1859   *The Absinthe Drinker* (Plate 2) is Manet's first submission to the Paris Salon. It is refused.

1860   Becomes friendly with Baudelaire.

1861   Success at the Salon with *Portrait of M. and Mme. Manet* (Fig. 5) and *The Spanish Singer* (Plate 3).

1863   Spring. *Le Déjeuner sur l'herbe* (Plate 8) and two other paintings are rejected by the Salon and hung in the 'notorious' Salon des Refusés. October 28. Marries – in Holland – Suzanne Leenhoff, who had been his mistress for more than ten years.

1865   *Olympia* (Plate 9) harshly criticized when shown at the Salon.

1866   Zola praises Manet's work in *L'Événement*.

1867   May. Partly as a snub to the Paris World Fair's official art exhibition, Manet shows fifty pictures in a temporary building put up at his own expense on the place de l'Alma.

1870   Serves in the Franco-Prussian War.

1872   Sells work to the dealer, Paul Durand-Ruel.

1879   Suggests to the authorities a plan to decorate the rebuilt Hôtel-de-Ville with scenes of contemporary life. The scheme is ignored.

1879   Autumn. Begins to suffer seriously from what was probably locomotor ataxia.

1881   December 30. Manet is made a Chevalier of the Legion of Honour.

1883   By beginning of April, Manet is bedridden. On the 30th he dies.

NOTES ON THE PLATES

1. THE BOY WITH THE CHERRIES (*L'Enfant aux Cerises*). 1858–60. Oil on canvas. $25\frac{3}{4} \times 21\frac{1}{2}$ in. Gulbenkian Foundation, Lisbon.
The model was a young boy named Alexandre who helped Manet in the studio and occasionally posed for him. The lad committed suicide in a moment of despair, and was the subject of a short story by Baudelaire, *La Corde*, in *Petits Poèmes en Prose*.

2. THE ABSINTHE-DRINKER (*Le Buveur d'absinthe*). 1858–9. Oil on canvas. $71\frac{1}{4} \times 41\frac{3}{4}$ in. Ny Carlsberg Glyptotek, Copenhagen.
Primarily of historical interest, Manet's first attempt at naturalism is bold, simple and well painted, but less original than the artist had hoped – 'Admit that I was entirely myself in *The Absinthe-Drinker*,' Manet besought Baudelaire; 'euh ! euh !' was the only reply. The subject derives from *Les Fleurs du Mal*, the idiom from Daumier and much of the technique from Couture. The model, Collardet, was a drunken rag-and-bone- man who hung around the Louvre. Manet made drawings and engravings of the same subject and reintroduced the figure into *The Old Musician* (Plate 4).

3. THE SPANISH SINGER, also called LE GUITARRERO (*Le Chanteur Espagnol*, ou *Le Guitarrero*). 1860. Oil on canvas. $58\frac{1}{2} \times 45\frac{3}{5}$ in. Metropolitan Museum (Gift of William Church Osborn, 1949), New York.
Although deriving from a print by Goya and Greuze's *Mandoliniste* (Louvre), which Manet probably knew from the engraving, the painting of *The Spanish Singer* must be seen as Manet's first truly original work and also as his first popular success. The famous Andalusian guitarist, Huerta, inspired this composition but did not sit for it, nor – *pace* Jamot-Wildenstein – did Jérôme Bosch (another popular guitarist), but an anonymous Sevillian model who was either left-handed or unable to hold a guitar. This shortcoming is remedied in a subsequent engraving in which the composition is reversed. A water-colour, which may be either a sketch for the present painting, or a reduction made after it (or even a try out for the engraving, which is almost the same size), is in the Eissler Collection, Vienna.

4. THE OLD MUSICIAN (*Le Vieux Musicien*). 1861–62. Oil on canvas. $74 \times 97\frac{1}{4}$ in. Chester Dale Collection, National Gallery of Art, Washington.
Manet's most ambitious work to date. The idea for the composition came from Goya's engraving after Velazquez' *Topers* (Prado) which Manet owned and which he introduced into his *Portrait of Zola* (Plate 24). Alas, despite magnificent passages of paint, the composition is far less homogeneous than the Velazquez. The violinist (Guéroult, 'an old Jew with a white beard') and some of the other models were discovered by Manet in a shanty-town ghetto in course of demolition known as 'Little Poland'.

5. MUSIC IN THE TUILERIES GARDENS (*La Musique aux Tuileries*). 1862. Oil on canvas. $30 \times 46\frac{1}{2}$ in. National Gallery, London.
The conception of this picture owes much to Baudelaire's thoughts (*see* Introduction) and it is significant that when making preliminary sketches for it – groups of nursemaids listening to the band – Manet was often accompanied by Baudelaire. Indeed the top-hatted artist, impassive behind his easel, and the heavily farded poet ('What genius lies under those layers of paint !', said Manet) caused a considerable stir on this fashionable promenade. Baudelaire can be discerned behind the seated woman (full-face) in the left foreground; Manet and his friend Albert de Balleroy are on the extreme left. Zacharie Astruc, Eugène Manet, Offenbach, Théophile Gautier, Fantin-Latour are also present.

6. THE STREET SINGER (*La Chanteuse des Rues*). 1862. Oil on canvas. $68\frac{1}{2} \times 46\frac{1}{2}$ in. Museum of Fine Arts, Boston.
Probably the earliest manifestation of the influence of Japanese prints in Manet's art.
Antonin Proust has described walking with Manet in an old part of Paris which was being demolished to make way for Baron Haussmann's new Malesherbes *quartier*. 'A woman stepped out of a low cabaret lifting up her dress and carrying a guitar. Manet went straight up to her and asked her to pose for him. She merely laughed. "I'll have another go," he said, "and if she doesn't want to, I'll use Victorine".' This, in the event, is what he did.
Victorine-Louise Meurent (born about 1842), the model for *Olympia*, *The Picnic* and *The Railway*, had the Baudelairean attributes – a serene expression and lithe physique – that Manet most liked to paint. A fantastic personality who painted and played the guitar, Victorine-Louise Meurent disappeared to America in mysterious circumstances in the 1860's, had an unfortunate romance and returned to Paris in the early 1870's, when she became temporarily Alfred Stevens' mistress. She continued to pose for Manet (e.g. Fig. 7), but later gave up modelling for painting, exhibiting a self-portrait at the 1876 Salon (Manet's works were rejected) and a *Nuremberg Bourgeoise of the XVIth century* in the same room as Manet in 1879. After losing money and looks, she used to hawk drawings in the street, took to drink and ended her life as a slattern called 'La Glu'.

7. LOLA DE VALENCE. 1862. Oil on canvas. $48\frac{3}{8}\times 36\frac{1}{4}$ in. Musée du Louvre, Paris.
The largest and finest of Manet's paintings of Camprubi's ballet company (*see* also note on Fig. 2) is this somewhat Goyesque portrait of the *première danseuse*. The background, originally plain, was altered 'on the advice of friends', but we know what it was like from Manet's engraved version, the third state of which is embellished with a quatrain by Baudelaire:

Entre tant de beautés que partout on peut voir
Je comprends bien, amis, que le désir balance,
Mais on voit scintiller dans Lola de Valence
Le charme inattendu d'un bijou rose et noir.

Manet also executed a lithograph after this portrait for the cover of a song written by Zacharie Astruc and dedicated to the Queen of Spain.

8. THE PICNIC (*Le Déjeuner sur l'Herbe*). 1862–63. Oil on canvas. $84\frac{3}{4}\times 106\frac{3}{8}$ in. Musée du Louvre, Paris.
Antonin Proust relates how one Sunday he and Manet were at Argenteuil watching the boats on the river: 'Some women were bathing. Manet had his eye fixed on the flesh of those coming out of the water. "It appears," he said, "that I must do a nude. Very well, I'll do one. When we were at Couture's I copied Giorgione's *Concert Champêtre*. It is black, that picture; the dark priming has come through. I want to do that over again in terms of transparent light and with people like these".' Victorine Meurent, Manet's brother Gustave and the Dutch sculptor Ferdinand Leenhoff (later his brother-in-law) were the models; the landscape was done from sketches made at Gennevilliers and Ile de Saint-Ouen. Manet based his composition on a detail from an engraving by Marcantonio Raimondi after Raphael's lost *Judgement of Paris*; this was first pointed out by Ernest Chesneau when the painting was exhibited in 1863 and not, as is usually claimed, by Gustav Pauli in 1908. A study in pencil and water colour in the Walzer Collection, Oxford, would seem to be a preliminary sketch; another in oils (Courtauld Institute Galleries, London) also exists – sometimes said to be a version done after the original. However, in both of these the Victorine Meurent figure has fair hair, whereas in No. 8 she is dark.

9. OLYMPIA. 1863. Oil on canvas, $51\frac{1}{8}\times 74\frac{3}{4}$ in. Musée du Louvre, Paris.
Posed by Victorine Meurent, christened by Zacharie Astruc who wrote a Baudelairean poem of 50 lines, *La Fille des Iles*, in honour of it. Titian's *Venus of Urbino*, which Manet had copied as a student (Coll. Rouart, Paris), influenced the composition (e.g. the vertical division of the background); there are also echoes of Goya's *Maja Desnuda* (Prado), Ingres' *Odalisque with the Slave* (Fogg Art Museum) and Jean Jalabert's *Odalisque* (Musée de Carcassonne), a popular academic set-piece of 1842 in which a black servant likewise figures. But *Olympia* entirely transcends earlier models and must be seen as one of the key-paintings of the XIXth century. Besides the water-colour in the Stavros Niarchos Collection, Paris, Manet executed several drawings and some engravings of this subject.

10. DETAIL OF PLATE 8.

11. DETAIL OF PLATE 9.

12. WOMEN AT THE RACES (*Les Courses*). 1864–5. Oil on canvas. $16\frac{5}{8}\times 12\frac{5}{8}$ in. Art Museum, Cincinnati.
It has been convincingly suggested by Harris (*Art Bulletin*, XLVIII, 1966, pp. 78–82) that this study and another fragment, *Women at the Races* (Jamot-Wildenstein, No. 115), originally formed part of a large painting which Manet exhibited at Martinet's Gallery in Paris in 1865, and afterwards cut up, and whose general character and appearance is recorded in the water-colour of 1864 in the Fogg Art Museum. The Cincinnati fragment is dated 1865, but this date was probably added after the large canvas was dismembered.

13. THE BATTLE OF THE KEARSARGE AND THE ALABAMA. 1864. Oil on canvas. $52\frac{3}{4}\times 50$ in. The John G. Johnson Collection, Philadelphia.
There is considerable argument as to whether this unusual painting, which depicts an episode in the American Civil War, was based on first hand experience: Proust claimed that Manet had been on board a pilot boat during the battle, but there is other evidence to suggest that he may not have been present at all.

14. THE DEAD TOREADOR (*Le Torero Mort*). 1863–64. Oil on canvas. $29\frac{1}{2}\times 60\frac{1}{2}$ in. National Gallery of Art, Washington.
Manet's *Bull-Fighting Episode* was so adversely criticised at the 1864 Salon for its excessive *Hispagnolisme* – 'Spanish dolls served up in a black sauce *à la Ribera* by M. Manet y Courbetos y Zurbaran de las Batignollas' – and for the disproportion of its various parts, that the artist cut out this and another passage and destroyed the rest of the composition. This figure is based on the so-called *Orlando Muerto* (National Gallery) – once thought to be by Velazquez – which Manet had presumably seen in the Pourtalès collection.

15. PEONIES (*Branche de Pivoines*). 1864. Oil on canvas. $12\frac{3}{8}\times 18\frac{1}{4}$ in. Musée du Louvre, Paris.
In 1864 Manet revealed himself as a masterly painter of still-lifes and flower-pieces. From the early summer of this year dates a series of nine flower-paintings, mostly of the peonies which grew in profusion at the artist's country property at Gennevilliers. Manet's still-lifes are usually very freshly and informally painted, as if he were relaxing from his more taxing experimental works.

16. BULL-FIGHTING SCENE (*Course de Taureaux*). 1865–66. Oil on canvas. 35⅜×43¼ in. Heirs of Baroness Goldschmidt-Rothschild, Paris.

'I have seen a superb bull-fight,' Manet wrote to Zacharie Astruc on his way back from Spain in 1865, 'and intend when I get back to Paris to pin down on canvas the appearance of this motley crowd of people, without forgetting the dramatic part, the picador and horse knocked down and savaged by the bull's horns and the army of *chulos* (assistants) trying to draw the furious animal away.' After his Spanish visit Manet painted three compositions, two small and sketchy ones (Art Institute, Chicago and Collection Matsukata, Tokyo) and this larger, more masterly work which vividly depicts what his letter describes.

17. THE EXECUTION OF MAXIMILIAN (*Exécution de Maximilien*). 1867–68. Oil on canvas. 99¼×120 in. Städtische Kunsthalle, Mannheim.

On June 19, 1867, Emperor Maximilian of Mexico and Generals Miramon and Mejia were executed by Mexican nationalists at Queretaro. Shortly afterwards Manet, who had been deeply moved by the violent death of this innocent, art-loving man, embarked on a vast composition depicting the incident. Basing himself on detailed newspaper reports and drawing on Goya's *Execution, May 3, 1808* (Prado) for compositional assistance, Manet painted first a large version (Museum of Fine Arts, Boston) which was never finished, secondly a large canvas which he cut up into three fragments (National Gallery, London), thirdly a small sketch (Ny Carlsberg Glyptotek, Copenhagen) and, finally, this culminant painting. Manet's lithograph of the same subject was banned by the authorities as being critical of the régime. Thus, this painting was not publicly shown until 1879–80, when Manet sent it to America.

18. PORTRAIT OF THÉODORE DURET. 1868. Oil on canvas. 18¼×14 in. Petit Palais, Paris.

Duret, a well-known art critic of the day, and a defender of the Impressionists, left a detailed account of the various sittings for this portrait (cf. Duret, *Histoire d'Édouard Manet et de son oeuvre*, 1902, pp. 35–7, 71–3). Whistler painted a life-size portrait of Duret dressed for the opera (1882–4, now in the Metropolitan Museum, New York), a presentation to which George Moore took exception, as being uncharacteristic: 'Did he [Whistler] ever see Duret in dress clothes? . . . Did he ever see Duret with an opera cloak? . . . But these facts mattered nothing to Whistler as they matter to Degas or to Manet. . . .'

19. THE FIFER (*Le Fifre*). 1866. Oil on canvas. 63×38½ in. Musée du Louvre, Paris.

Manet's military friend, Commandant Lejosne, arranged for a young fife-player of the *Garde Impériale* to have special leave to pose for this figure. The features are sometimes said to be those of Victorine Meurent, but this cannot be true, as her ears were not so big, nor were her eyes so widely spaced;

only the dead-pan' expression is reminiscent of her. Tabarant's suggestion that Léon Koëlla (Manet's stepson) posed for the face is more probable. Note influence of Japanese prints, in the stylization and lack of modelling, and of Velazquez, in 'the way the figure is surrounded by nothing but air' – the quality that Manet so admired in *Pablillos de Valladolid*. A key-work for Manet's synthesis of Spanish and Japanese elements.

20. THE READING (*La Lecture*). 1869. Oil on canvas. 24×29⅝ in. Musée du Louvre, Paris.

Mme. Manet is being read to by her son, Léon Koëlla, in their Paris apartment. Suzanne Leenhoff (1830–1906) had originally taught the painter and his younger brothers music. However, even Manet's most intimate friends did not know that this plump Dutch girl had been his mistress for more than ten years before she married him in Holland in 1863; and it is still unclear whether Mme. Manet's son, who went by the name of Léon Édouard Koëlla (1852–1927) and passed for her younger brother until after Manet's death, was the son of the artist or of someone else (no Koëlla being traceable). Manet painted his wife several times between 1858 and 1880. In 1868, for example, he depicted her playing the piano (Paris, Louvre).

21. LUNCHEON IN THE STUDIO (*Le Déjeuner dans l'Atelier*). 1868. Oil on canvas. 47¼×60⅝ in. Bayerische Staatsgemäldesammlungen (Neue Staatsgalerie), Munich.

In the summer of 1868 the Manets took a house at Boulogne-sur-mer – 'Scantily furnished with souvenirs belonging to the old sea-dog who rented it to us,' said Koëlla – and there in the dining-room Manet made an oil sketch (since lost) which was the point of departure for this masterpiece subsequently painted in Paris. The youth is Léon Koëlla; the man on the right is Auguste Rousselin, a painter whom Manet had known at Couture's; the maid a girl from Boulogne. The composition – unusually elaborate and successful for Manet – is reminiscent of Degas' *Bellelli Family* (Louvre) of 1860–62.

22. STILL LIFE WITH SALMON (*Le Saumon*). 1866–9. Oil on canvas. 29×37 in. The Electra Havemeyer Webb Fund, Shelburne Museum, Shelburne, Vermont.

23. DETAIL OF PLATE 21.

24. PORTRAIT OF ÉMILE ZOLA. 1867–68. Oil on canvas. 57×43⅝ in. Musée du Louvre, Paris.

The landscape painter, Antonin Guillemet, brought Emile Zola (1840–1902) to see Manet in February, 1866. Much impressed by the man as well as by his art, Zola wrote an enthusiastic defence of Manet's work (*L'Événement*, May 7, 1866), later expanded into a long article (*Revue du XIXe Siècle*, January 1, 1867). Full of gratitude, Manet painted this portrait of Zola, who posed seven or eight times between November, 1867 and February, 1868. Note inclusion of

Utamaro print, photograph of *Olympia* and engraving after Velazquez' *Topers*. The revolutionary painting of the face as a flatly lit, unmodelled area scandalized visitors to the 1868 Salon. Note how characterization has been sacrificed to stylistic consideration.

25. EVA GONZALÈS. 1870. Oil on canvas. 75×51½ in. National Gallery, London.

Eva Gonzalès (1849–83) was a painter of Spanish descent who entered Manet's studio as his pupil in February, 1869. According to Tabarant, Manet began a portrait of her at this time; it proved difficult and was not completed until March, 1870. When shown at the Manet Exhibition of 1884, it was framed with all four corners rounded. Eva Gonzalès, who was also the subject of a Manet etching of 1870, married Henri Guérard in 1879. The present portrait is featured in Orpen's portrait group, *Homage to Manet* (City Art Gallery, Manchester).

26. RACECOURSE IN THE BOIS DE BOULOGNE (*Courses aux Bois de Boulogne*). 1872. Oil on canvas. 28¾×36¼ in. Collection Mr. John Hay Whitney, New York.

After visiting his parents-in-law in Holland in the summer of 1872, Manet embarked on this painting, commissioned by Monsieur Barret, the sportsman and collector. On October 21, Manet wrote to say it was finished and the following day sent a receipt for 3,000 francs. Degas prided himself on having painted racecourse scenes before Manet (as early as 1860–62) – a fact which Manet seems to acknowledge by including a likeness of Degas in the bottom right-hand corner of this work. Unlike Degas, who knew from experience exactly how a horse's body was articulated, Manet copied his stylized animals from English sporting-prints. 'Not being in the habit of painting horses,' he said to Berthe Morisot, 'I copied mine from those who know best how to do them.' Note contrast between sharp focus of horses and impressionistic handling of crowd and Saint-Cloud hillside.

27. THE HARBOUR AT BORDEAUX (*Le Port de Bordeaux*). 1871. Oil on canvas. 24¾×39⅜ in. Collection Heirs of Emil Bührle, Zurich.

After the armistice in February, 1871, Manet rejoined his family who had taken refuge with friends at Oloron in south-west France. They decided to take a villa at Arcachon for the month of March, but before going there spent a week in Bordeaux, where the newly elected *Assemblée Nationale* was sitting. From the window of a café on the Quai des Chartrons, Manet did a preliminary water-colour and then this magnificent painting – his most ambitious marine subject. Note similarity to some of Boudin's Le Havre scenes of the 1860's and some of Jongkind's harbour views for which Manet had a high regard. Manet's hero, Gambetta, greatly admired this picture but refused to accept it as a present.

28. ARGENTEUIL. 1874. Oil on canvas. 58⅝×51½ in. Musée des Beaux-Arts, Tournai.

It is almost incredible that *Argenteuil* once seemed shocking, but when it was exhibited at the 1875 Salon, a typical comment was: 'the indigo river is flat as a wall . . . Argenteuil looks like pulp.' Manet's only consolation was that a minority of critics (including the formidable Chesneau) realized that the brilliant blue, instead of being out of tone, made the painting vibrate with summer light and that his *Argenteuil* was a serious attempt to depict contemporary life. The same yachtsman afterwards posed for *Sailing* (*En Bateau*), the well-known canvas, also of 1874, now in the Metropolitan Museum, New York. His identity is not certain. Tabarant and Jamot-Wildenstein agree that he was Rudolph Leenhoff (1844–1903), Madame Manet's painter brother. But J. E. Blanche, who knew Manet well, maintained that Baron Barbier – an enthusiastic yachtsman and intimate friend of Guy de Maupassant – was the model.

29. THE GRAND CANAL, VENICE (*Le Grand Canal à Venise*). 1874. Oil on canvas. 22½×18⅞ in. Property of the Provident Securities Company, San Francisco.

In September 1874 Manet went to Venice with James Tissot, the French *genre* painter who lived in London. Two views, the present one and the horizontal picture now in the Shelburne Museum, Vt., were probably painted from the Palazzo Barbaro which belonged to a rich American amateur called Curtis (a close friend of Sargent and later of Monet). Certainly the Shelburne picture (subsequently bought by Tissot) corresponds to a view across the Grand Canal which Monet painted from this *palazzo* in 1908; only the buildings in the left background were presumably done from memory, for they neither look Venetian nor fit with the rest of the scene. No. 29 is a view down the Canal towards the Dogana, with the dome of the Salute in the background. Note the dappled impressionistic brushwork in both paintings. According to J. E. Blanche, these works were also known as *Les Palibleus*.

30. THE GAME OF CROQUET (*La Partie de Croquet*). 1873. Oil on canvas. 28½×41¾ in. Städelsches Kunstinstitut, Frankfurt.

Painted in Alfred Stevens' large Paris garden, the scene of frequent croquet parties. On the left is Victorine Meurent; on the right Alice Lecouvé (Stevens' model); in the background Paul Roudier, the artist's old friend, who also appears in an earlier croquet picture (Tabarant, No. 180) done at Boulogne in 1871; the man in the foreground is possibly Stevens. Note how the figures seem casually placed but are in fact carefully disposed to suggest recession. The paint is applied in an impressionist manner, but the colour is not broken up prismatically, as in comparable pictures by Renoir or Monet. After being lost for years, this canvas was rediscovered in a Berne junkshop by the actor Dorival.

31. THE RIVER AT ARGENTEUIL (*Bords de la Seine à Argenteuil*). 1874. Oil on canvas. 24×38⅜ in. The Dowager Lady Aberconway, London.

A view from Gennevilliers across to Argenteuil. The woman and child have not been identified, but might be Madame Monet and her son Jean. The white structure in the background is a floating bathing establishment. The three boats moored in midstream re-appear in another smaller canvas (Tabarant No. 228). The subject and *facture* are typically impressionist, though not the colour which is mixed with black instead of being broken down into spectral constituents; hence this painting is less luminous than comparable views by Monet and Renoir.

32. NUDE (*Femme nue en buste*). 1875. Oil on canvas. 24×19⅖ in. Musée du Louvre, Paris.

Although featured in two of his most famous and important paintings, the *Déjeuner sur l'Herbe* (Plate 8) and *Olympia* (Plate 9), the female nude is actually quite rare in Manet's work, partly, one suspects, because he found that clothing offered more varied and interesting textures to paint than flesh. And certainly his treatment of flesh lacks Renoir's exquisite translucence.

33. SPRING: JEANNE (*Le Printemps – Jeanne*). 1881. Oil on canvas. 28¾×20 in. Collection Mrs. Harry Payne Bingham, New York.

In 1876 Alfred Stevens was commissioned by the King of the Belgians to paint four fashionable beauties symbolizing the seasons; this fact was certainly known to Manet and probably decided him to do the same. That the artist only completed half the series is particularly regrettable, for this and *Autumn: Méry Laurent* (Nancy, Museum) are two of his finest late portraits; *Spring* was also his first great Salon success (1882). An engraving by Manet of this painting exists as well as a drawing (Fogg Art Museum) which is interesting in being executed over a faint photographic base corresponding to the present work. It is typical of Manet that he took his model – a young actress called Jeanne de Marsy – to a well-known milliner (Madame Virot) to buy a hat for the occasion that would be appropriately spring-like and ultra-fashionable. Manet also considered painting a series of allegorical figures of the wines of France: 'a brunette for Burgundy; a red-head for claret; a blonde for champagne.'

34. THE ARTIST (*Portrait of Gilbert-Marcellin Desboutin*). 1875. Oil on canvas. 76×51 in. Museum of Art, São Paulo.

Gilbert-Marcellin Desboutin (1823–1902) – engraver, painter, dramatist and art-dealer – was as picturesque in character as in appearance. Having spent most of his patrimony on a handsome property, L'Ombrellino, outside Florence, he lived by dealing in old masters After 1870 he returned to Paris, more or less broke, but had considerable success with his portraits, especially the engraved ones (e.g.

some excellent studies of Manet of 1876). A water-colour sketch of the same sitter exists (Tabarant No. 617). 'My aim has not been to epitomize a period,' said Manet of this portrait, 'but to depict an exceptional personality.' Compare portraits of Desboutin by Degas, Boldini and other contemporary artists.

35. NANA. 1877. Oil on canvas. 59×45⅝ in. Kunsthalle, Hamburg.

Always a stickler for naturalism, Manet arranged for a *grande cocotte* Henriette Hauser to pose for this 'slice of contemporary life'. A success in musical comedy (notably as *Fée Coquette*), Henriette Hauser was kept by the Prince of Orange – hence her nickname *Citron*. The admirer in this picture has not been identified. For the occasion Manet arranged a corner of his studio as a dressing-room, fixing up special heating so that his model could pose *en déshabillé*. While *Nana* was being painted, Zola's novel with the same title and theme was appearing, but this seems to have been a coincidence. Rejected, on moral grounds, by the Salon Jury in 1877, *Nana* was exhibited in Giroux' fashionable shop (Boulevard des Capucines) with such *succès de scandale* that the police were called in.

36. THE PLUM (*La Prune*). 1877. Oil on canvas. 29⅛×19¼ in. Collection Mr. and Mrs. Paul Mellon, Upperville, Virginia.

After a period devoted mostly to portraits and impressionist *motifs*, Manet resumed in 1877 being 'the painter of modern life.' *The Plum*, *Skating* and *Nana* were all conceived, according to Tabarant, as 'naturalistic subjects'. The model for this work has not been identified, but the setting is said to be the Café de la Nouvelle Athènes – a favourite rendezvous of Manet and his friends. Note the influence of Degas whose *Absinthe* (Louvre), painted the year before, also depicts a drab slumped in front of a café table. Note also how a panel of *art nouveau* decoration is used to convey period feeling.

37. DETAIL OF PLATE 38.

38. THE ROAD-MENDERS, RUE DE BERNE (*Les Paveurs, rue de Berne*). 1878. Oil on canvas. 25×31½ in. Collection Lord Butler, London.

Before moving from his studio (4, rue Saint-Petersbourg), Manet recorded the view from his window on to the rue Mosnier (now rue de Berne), first making preliminary drawings (Museum of Fine Arts, Budapest, and Art Institute, Chicago) for the composition and oil sketches of the cab and a figure by a lamp-post. This is one of Manet's most successful paintings in the impressionist idiom – less atmospheric but more tangibly Parisian than Monet's *Gare Saint-Lazare* series of the year before. Later in the summer, when Paris was decorated for a *Fête Nationale* (June 30, 1878) in honour of the Exposition Universelle, Manet painted two further views (Colls. Paul Mellon,

Upperville, Va., and Bührle, Zurich) of the rue Mosnier decked with flags. Cf. two similar views of decorated streets which Monet painted on the same occasion.

39. AT THE CAFÉ (*Cabaret de Reichshoffen*). 1878. Oil on canvas. 30¾×33 in. Stiftung Dr. Oskar Reinhart, Winterthur. See No. 46.

40. AT PÈRE LATHUILLE'S (*Chez le Père Lathuille*). 1879. Oil on canvas. 36⅜×44⅛ in. Musée des Beaux-Arts, Tournai. Almost next door to the Café Guerbois – the headquarters of 'la bande à Manet' – was the excellent restaurant, *Chez le Père Lathuille*. Louis Gauthier-Lathuille, the son of the proprietor, has described the origins of this picture: '. . . in July, 1879, when on leave from military service, I met Manet outside our house. He admired my appearance and said to my father, "I have an idea. I am going to paint your son as a dragoon." He got Ellen Andrée to come – young, sweet, amusing, dressed to kill . . . It was charming. The picture came along fine . . . There were two sittings, Manet carefully putting aside his canvas when the first clients arrived for lunch. But at the third sitting, no Ellen Andrée . . . The day after, she reappeared, but a bit late . . . she had been rehearsing. Furious, Manet decided to get rid of her . . . The next day I saw him arrive with Judith French, a relation of Offenbach's. I took up the same pose with her, but it was not the same thing. Manet appeared nervous. "Take off your uniform," he finally said, "and put on my smock" . . . That's how it came about that I posed as a civilian with Mlle. French.' *At Père Lathuille's* is one of Manet's most brilliant and Maupassant-like vignettes of contemporary life.

41. VILLA AT RUEIL (*La Maison de Rueil*). 1882. Oil on canvas. 36¼×28½ in. National Gallery of Victoria, Melbourne.
Manet spent the summer of 1882 at Rueil near Malmaison; again he loathed being away from Paris and having to paint a suburban garden. The decline in his health did not, however, affect his technique, and the two views of the villa – this and a horizontal version (Staatliche Museen, Berlin) – show that Manet's outdoor scenes can be as fresh as Monet's or Renoir's. Only the brilliance of sunlight, which the Impressionists conjured up with complementary colours, is lacking. Manet did six other, mostly rather sketchy, paintings of the garden at Rueil.

42. PORTRAIT OF HENRI ROCHEFORT. 1881. Oil on canvas. 32⅛×26⅛ in. Kunsthalle, Hamburg.
Condemned under military law to life imprisonment for the part he played in the Commune, Henri Rochefort (1830–1913; born Marquis de Rochefort-Luçay) was transported to a penal settlement in New Caledonia. After escaping by boat with a few others in 1874, he lived in London and Geneva until the general amnesty allowed him to return to France in 1880. Out of hero-worship, Manet painted two

pictures of the escape (Tabarant, Nos. 374 and 375) and this portrait, which Rochefort – no liker of modern painting – refused. Ironically, this passionate Radical (founder of *L'Intransigeant*) ultimately became a follower of General Boulanger and leader of the anti-Dreyfusards.

43. PORTRAIT OF MADAME MICHEL LÉVY. 1882. Pastel. 29¼×21¾ in. Chester Dale Collection, National Gallery of Art, Washington.
Manet had first experimented with pastels in the early 1870's (e.g. *Madame Manet on a sofa*, 1874, Louvre, Paris), but he only started working consistently in the medium – an easy one for an invalid to handle – when he could no longer stand at an easel. The technique which he evolved between 1878 and his death in 1883 derives not, as one might imagine, from Degas, but from XVIIIth-century pastellists (Quentin de la Tour, Perronneau, etc.) whose light and pretty works are often surprisingly free and daringly coloured. Manet did more than 50 pastel portraits; a few of men (Guys, Chabrier, Moore, etc.), most of young and pretty women – sometimes *grandes cocottes* (Méry Laurent or Irma Brunner), sometimes, as here, *femmes du monde*. Madame Michel Lévy was the wife of a publisher who was also a collector of modern paintings. Manet executed two portraits of her (both commissioned), the second (Tabarant No. 533) being a sketchy oval version of the present work.

44. INTERIOR OF A CAFÉ (*Interieur de Café*). c. 1880. Oil and pastel on linen. 12¾×18 in. City Art Gallery, Glasgow (Burrell Collection).
One of a number of café scenes, dating from the last years of Manet's life, of which Plate 45 is the most important.

45. A BAR AT THE FOLIES-BERGÈRE (*Un bar aux Folies-Bergère*). 1881–2. Oil on canvas. 37¾×51⅛ in. Courtauld Institute Galleries, London (Home House Trustees).
Manet's culminant work and last great evocation of contemporary life. As in the 1860's, the artist chose an impassively pretty *fille du peuple* to epitomize the spirit of his period. But *The Bar* is more imaginatively composed and richly painted (note especially the still-life) than earlier works; and Manet has taken more daring liberties than in the 1860's; note that the reflections of the girl's back and the man (on the left) do not accord with the frontal view but are nevertheless pictorially convincing. The model was a barmaid called Suzon (subsequently the mistress of Manet's biographer, Bazire); she also posed for another painting and a pastel (Tabarant Nos. 398 and 504). The man on the right is Henry Dupray (1841–1909); Méry Laurent (in white) and the painter Gaston Latouche are also reflected in the mirror. Manet made several preliminary notes, most of them unpublished (*Dessins et Aquarelles d'Édouard Manet, Album No. 5*; sold at Galerie Charpentier, Paris, June 10, 1954), a water-colour study (whereabouts unknown) and an oil sketch (Coll. Koenigs, Haarlem), largely repainted by another hand, of a blonde barmaid talking to Dupray.

46. THE WAITRESS (*La Servante de Bocks*). 1878. Oil on canvas. 30¼×24¼ in. Musée du Louvre, Paris.
In 1878 Manet continued to paint naturalistic subjects: eight canvases and numerous drawings of cabaret and *café-chantant* scenes, including a large *Brasserie de Reichshoffen* begun in August. The artist is said to have cut this into two fragments: No. 39 and a larger version of No. 46 (National Gallery, London). But how these two parts formed a single coherent composition is a mystery, since, even if we allow for subsequent re-working, the scale and position of the various figures are hardly reconcilable. *Pace* Mr. Martin Davies, who has made a very thorough investigation of the problem (*National Gallery – Catalogue of the French School*, 2nd Ed.), the present writer feels that No. 46 is more likely to be the missing half of No. 39. The bearded man in No. 39 is Henri Guérard who in 1879 married Manet's pupil, Eva Gonzalès; the girl with him is the actress Ellen Andrée; the third figure has not been identified. Manet also did a sketch for the two central figures (Tabarant No. 295). The model for No. 46 was one of the waitresses at the Brasserie Reich-shoffen who insisted that her *galant* – the man in the blue blouse – accompany her when she posed. Cf. a lithograph with a similar subject, *Les Chinois de Paris No. I* (1863) by Daumier.

47. DETAIL OF PLATE 45.

48. LILAC (*Un Bouquet de Lilas*). 1883. Oil on canvas. 21½×16½ in. Nationalgalerie, Berlin-Charlottenburg.
Manet's studio had always been full of flowers but never so full as during his last illness. The bouquets, which Méry Laurent and other friends sent, were a source of constant visual pleasure and inspired a series of exquisite flower pieces (1882–3). True, these are less adventurous than earlier works, but they are as fresh and delicate as anything Manet ever did and should be seen as *beaux morceaux de peinture* in the great French tradition of Chardin and Fragonard. No. 48 is one of the last works that Manet painted.

Frontispiece. THE BALCONY (*Le Balcon*). 1868. Oil on canvas. 66½×48½ in. Musée du Louvre, Paris.
As so often with Manet (e.g. *The Picnic*), the stimulus of a thing seen – in this case a group of people on a balcony at Boulogne – combined with the memory of a painting by an earlier master – in this case Goya's *Women on the Balcony* (Prado) – were the starting point for an original work of art. Berthe Morisot (1840–95), chaperoned by her mother, posed for the girl in the foreground; Fanny Claus, a violinist, for the girl on the right (cf. a separate study; coll. Pitman, London); and Antonin Guillemet for the man. Léon Koëlla can be discerned in the background holding a tray. A letter (March, 1869), written by Berthe Morisot's mother, describes the sitters' feelings: 'Antonin says that Manet has got him to pose fifteen times, only to make a botch of things and that Mlle. Claus is atrocious; however, the two of them were so exhausted with posing in a standing-position that they said, "it's perfect, nothing needs touching".' The group is charming and each figure is masterly, but there is no bond, no thematic link between them; each stares fixedly out at something different. Here is none of the intimacy and intensity of the Goya.

In text. MARGUERITE DE CONFLANS WEARING A HOOD (*Marguerite de Conflans au capuchon*). 1873. Oil on canvas. 21⅞×18¼ in. Stiftung Dr. Oskar Reinhart, Winterthur.
Marguerite de Conflans (later Madame d'Angély) came of a family which had close links with the Manets. A frequent guest at Madame Manet's musical parties, this striking, rather than pretty, girl so attracted the artist that he painted five portraits of her (Tabarant Nos. 212–215 *bis*), mostly in ball dress, as here. Manet worked at the Conflans' house; a *fille de bonne famille* could not go alone to the artist's studio.

ILLUSTRATIONS IN THE TEXT

1. A GROUP OF THIRTEEN CAVALIERS. c. 1860. Engraving heightened with water-colour. 9⅝×15¼ in. Present whereabouts unknown.
As well as this engraving, Manet also made a painted copy of *Les Petits Cavaliers* (Louvre, Paris), which in the 19th century was thought to be by Velazquez and to represent the Spanish master himself and twelve other celebrated artists, including Murillo. 'It is cleanly painted,' Manet said of it, 'that's what disgusts one with all the stews and gravy.' Certainly its free, easy grouping influenced Manet's compositions (e.g. Plate 5 and Fig. 2). Usually said to have been executed in the mid-1850s, this copy (Private Collection, U.S.A.) is more confidently handled than *The Absinthe Drinker* and therefore seems to date from 1860 – the year when it was probably engraved. Fig. 1 shows the first, slightly damaged state of the engraving. In order to cover up faulty passages and also perhaps to try out certain effects for the second state, Manet heightened the print with water-colour.

2. THE SPANISH DANCERS (*Le Ballet Espagnol*). 1862. Oil on canvas. 24×35¾ in. Phillips Memorial Gallery, Washington.
From August 12th until November 2nd, 1862, Mariano Camprubi's company of Spanish dancers performed with great success in Paris at the Hippodrome in a ballet called *Flor de Sevilla*. Manet made preliminary notes in the theatre, then had the company pose in Alfred Stevens' spacious studio; but the finished composition looks pieced together; also, because of the artist's fallible sense of pro-

portion, the central quartet appears strangely diminished. All the same, a lively and natural work.

3. THE PHILOSOPHER, WITH A BERET (*Le Philosophe*). 1865. Oil on canvas. 74¼ × 43 in. Art Institute, Chicago.
This and the companion painting, *The Philosopher, with a Hat* (also in the Art Institute, Chicago), were painted under the influence of the Velazquez canvases that Manet saw in the Prado, and in particular the *Aesop* and the *Menippus*.

4. MLLE. VICTORINE IN THE COSTUME OF AN ESPADA (*Mlle. Victorine en costume d'un Espada*). 1862. Oil on canvas. 65 × 50¼ in. New York, Metropolitan Museum.
As yet Manet had never seen a bull-fight and so, for all its charm, this costume-piece carries none of the conviction of his future tauromachic pictures of 1865–66. Here is simply a pretty Parisienne 'posing (as Douglas Cooper has said) against an appropriate backcloth and miming the matador's gestures with the *espièglerie* of a courtesan.' The disproportionately small bull-fighting scene is made up of elements borrowed from Goya's *Tauromaquia*.

5. PORTRAIT OF MONSIEUR AND MADAME AUGUSTE MANET. 1860. Oil on canvas. 44 × 36 in. Private Collection, Paris.
Manet always kept this painting hanging in his studio.

6. LE BON BOCK (*Le Bon Bock*). 1873. Oil on canvas. 37¼ × 32¾ in. Philadelphia Museum of Art (Mr. and Mrs. Carroll S. Tyson, Jr. Collection).
Shown at the Salon of 1873, and much admired, *Le Bon Bock* was painted after a visit to Holland in the summer of 1872; and it is very much a genre-piece in the Dutch manner.

7. THE RAILWAY (*Le Chemin de Fer*). 1873. Oil on canvas. 36⅝ × 44⅛ in. National Gallery of Art, Washington. (Gift of Horace Havemeyer.)
Manet's rue Saint-Petersbourg studio was so close to the Pont de l'Europe – the railway-bridge that partly appears on the right-hand edge of this work – that 'the floor trembled underfoot and shuddered like the deck of a ship at sea.' The background of this picture was painted in the studio from notes made in the immediate neighbourhood; the figures were done in a nearby garden belonging to Alphonse Hirsch, the artist. Hirsch's daughter posed for the child, Victorine Meurent for the woman. Manet was fascinated by railways, which he saw as an essentially modern phenomenon. 'One day coming back from Versailles,' he told Georges Jeanniot, 'I travelled on the engine with the driver and fireman. What a magnificent spectacle these two men were, what *sang-froid*, what guts! It's a dog's life. These men are modern heroes. When I am better, I will paint them.' Probably the picture which prompted Monet to paint a series of railway scenes, including one of the Pont de l'Europe (Paris, Musée Marmottan) three years later.

8. PORTRAIT OF STÉPHANE MALLARMÉ. 1876. Oil on canvas. 10⅝ × 13¾ in. Musée du Louvre, Paris.
The friendship between Manet and Mallarmé (1842–98) dates from about 1873. In April, 1874 the poet wrote an enthusiastic article about the artist; in 1875 Manet illustrated Mallarmé's translation of Poe's *Raven*, and his *L'Après-midi d'un faune* in 1876, by which time the poet and artist were seeing one another every day. Thus Mallarmé stepped into the place that Baudelaire had once occupied in the artist's life. According to Paul Valéry (a relation by marriage), Manet owed his fulfilment as an artist in great part to the stimulus of these two poets. One of Manet's most affectionate and perceptive portraits, this was executed in a single sitting; a narrow strip of canvas was later added on the right to balance the composition. Cf. the portraits of Mallarmé by Renoir and Gauguin.

9. SELF-PORTRAIT WITH PALETTE (*Manet à la Palette*). 1879. Oil on canvas. 32⅝ × 26⅜ in. Collection John L. Loeb, New York.
Manet painted two self-portraits at this time, the present work and a full-length composition (Tabarant No. 321), both undistinguished and lacking in self-analysis. Here we see Manet in the role of an elegant *boulevardier* for whom painting would seem to be no more than a pastime. The other presents a haggard and sick-looking man, a prey to the locomotor ataxia which was soon to kill him.

10. PORTRAIT OF GEORGE MOORE. 1879. Pastel. 21⅝ × 13¼ in. Metropolitan Museum, New York.
George Moore (1852–1933) came to study art in Paris in 1873 but soon decided to become a writer; he met Manet early in 1879 at the Café de la Nouvelle Athènes and frequently visited his studio. Yet, for all his pretension, Moore never understood or appreciated the painting of Manet or the Impressionists, most of what he wrote about his so-called friends being incorrect or unjust. Manet, however, was sufficiently diverted by this 'magnificent young Montmartrois with a blond beard *à la Capoul*' to do three portraits of him, all of 1879: this one (known by Manet's friends as *Le Noyé Repêché* – the man fished out of the water); the unfinished study of Moore in a café (Metropolitan Museum, New York); and a small seated figure study (Collection of Kurt Riezler, New York). It is significant that Moore never owned any of his own portraits by Manet.

11. MADAME EDOUARD MANET IN THE CONSERVATORY (*Madame Edouard Manet dans la Serre*). 1879. Oil on canvas. 32⅛ × 39⅜ in. National Gallery, Oslo.
So captivated was Manet by the conservatory at Rosen's studio that he followed up *In the Conservatory*, the carefully finished canvas now in Berlin, with this study of his wife in the same setting. The handling is much fresher and looser than in the Berlin painting – qualities that appeal to us today,

but which prompted Manet's contemporaries to complain that he was unable to finish a picture. A second version (Jamot-Wildenstein, No. 298; Coll. Bomford, London) is a coarse work and, as Tabarant maintains, more likely to be by Edouard Vibert (Madame Manet's nephew) whose copies of his uncle's paintings are often passed off as originals.

12. WOMAN FASTENING HER GARTER (*Femme à la Jarretiere*) – detail. About 1878. Pastel. 20⅞ × 17¼ in. Wilhelm Hansen Museum, Ordrupsgaard.

13. WOMAN WASHING HERSELF (*Femme dans un tub*). About 1878. Pastel, 21⅝ × 17¾ in. Collection Bernheim-Jeune, Paris.

According to Tabarant, the same model, Marguérite, posed for these two and three other related pastels, as well as for two paintings, all of 1878. However, the girl's hair is sometimes long and brown and sometimes short and fair, so it would seem that two different models were involved, the second perhaps being the Amelie-Jeanne mentioned by Madame Manet (*see* Tabarant, p. 320). This group of nude and *déshabillé* subjects, seemingly inspired by Degas, is exceptional in Manet's later work, for after *Olympia* he virtually renounced the nude, preferring to paint models in fashionable clothes that evoked the period. A horizontal, more sketchy version of Fig. 13, is in Coll. Schocken, Scarsdale, New York.

SELECTED BIBLIOGRAPHY

Duret, Théodore, *Histoire d'Édouard Manet et de son oeuvre*. Paris, H. Floury, 1902.

Proust, Antonin, *Édouard Manet: Souvenirs*. A. Barthélemey, H. Laurens, 1913.

Moreau-Nelaton, Étienne, *Manet: Graveur et lithographe*. Paris, L. Delteil, 1906.

Moreau-Nelaton, Étienne, *Manet raconté par lui-même* (2 vols.). Paris, Laurens, 1926.

Jamot, Paul, and Wildenstein, Georges, *Manet* (2 vols.). Paris, Beaux-Arts, 1932.

Tabarant, Adolphe, *Manet et ses oeuvres*. Paris, Gallimard, 1947.

Sandblad, Nils Gösta, *Manet: Three Studies in Artistic Conception*, Lund, CWK Gleerup, 1954.

Rewald, John, *History of Impressionism*. New York, Museum of Modern Art, 2nd edition, 1961.

Catalogue of Manet Exhibition, Philadelphia/Chicago, 1966/7.

LIST OF COLLECTIONS